An admirable statement of the aims of the Library of Philosophy was provided by the first editor, the late Professor J. H. Muirhead, in his description of the original programme printed in Erdmann's *History of Philosophy* under the date 1890. This was slightly modified in subsequent volumes to take the form of the following statement:

'The Muirhead Library of Philosophy was designed as a contribution to the History of Modern Philosophy under the heads: first of Different Schools of Thought—Sensationalist, Realist, Idealist, Intuitivist; secondly of different Subjects—Psychology, Ethics, Aesthetics, Political Philosophy, Theology. While much had been done in England in tracing the course of evolution in nature, history, economics, morals and religion, little had been done in tracing the development of thought on these subjects. Yet "the evolution of opinion is part of the whole evolution".

'By the co-operation of different writers in carrying out this plan it was hoped that a thoroughness and completeness of treatment, otherwise unattainable, might be secured. It was believed also that from writers mainly British and American fuller consideration of English Philosophy than it had hitherto received might be looked for. In the earlier series of books containing, among others, Bosanquet's *History of Aesthetic*, Pfleiderer's *Rational Theology since Kant*, Albee's *History of English Utilitarianism*, Bonar's *Philosophy and Political Economy*, Brett's *History of Psychology*, Ritchie's *Natural Rights*, these objects were to a large extent effected.

'In the meantime original work of a high order was being produced both in England and America by such writers as Bradley, Stout, Bertrand Russell, Baldwin, Urban, Montague, and others, and a new interest in foreign works, German, French and Italian, which had either become classical or were attracting public attention, had developed. The scope of the Library thus became extended into something more international, and it is entering on the fifth decade of its existence in the hope that it may contribute to that mutual understanding between countries which is so pressing a need of the present time.'

The need which Professor Muirhead stressed is no less pressing today, and few will deny that philosophy has much to do with enabling us to meet it, although no one, least of all Muirhead himself, would regard that as the sole, or even the main, object of philosophy. As Professor Muirhead continues to lend the distinction of his name to the Library of Philosophy it seemed not inappropriate to allow him to recall us to these aims in his own words. The emphasis on the history of thought also seemed to me very timely; and the number of important works promised for the Library in the very near future augur well for the continued fulfilment, in this and other ways, of the expectations of the original editor.

H. D. LEWIS

MUIRHEAD LIBRARY OF PHILOSOPHY

General Editor: H. D. Lewis

Professor of History and Philosophy of Religion in the University of London

Action by SIR MALCOLM KNOX
The Analysis of Mind by BERTRAND RUSSELL
Belief by H. H. PRICE
Brett's History of Psychology edited by R. S. PETERS
Clarity is Not Enough by H. D. LEWIS
Coleridge as a Philosopher by J. H. MUIRHEAD
The Commonplace Book of G. E. Moore edited by C. LEWY
Contemporary American Philosophy edited by C. P. ADAMS and W. P. MONTAGUE
Contemporary American Philosophy second series edited by JOHN E. SMITH
Contemporary British Philosophy first and second series edited by J. H. MUIRHEAD
Contemporary British Philosophy third series edited by H. D. LEWIS
Contemporary Indian Philosophy edited by RADHAKRISHNAN and J. H. MUIRHEAD 2nd edition
Contemporary Philosophy in Australia edited by ROBERT BROWN and C. D. ROLLINS
The Discipline of the Cave by J. N. FINDLAY
Doctrine and Argument in Indian Philosophy by NINIAN SMART
Ethics and Christianity by KEITH WARD
Essays in Analysis by ALICE AMBROSE
Ethical Knowledge by JOEL J. KUPPERMAN
Ethics by NICOLAI HARTMANN translated by STANTON COIT 3 vols
The Foundations of Metaphysics in Science by ERROL E. HARRIS
Freedom and History by H. D. LEWIS
The Good Will: A Study in the Coherence Theory of Goodness by H. J. PATON
Hegel: A Re-examination by J. N. FINLAY
Hegel's Science of Logic translated by W. H. JOHNSTON and L. G. STRUTHERS 2 vols
History of Aesthetic by B. BOSANQUET 2nd edition
History of English Utilitarianism by E. ALBEE
Human Knowledge by BERTRAND RUSSELL
A Hundred Years of British Philosophy by RUDOLF METZ translated by J. N. HARVEY, T. E. JESSOP, HENRY STURT
Ideas: A General Introduction to Pure Phenomenology by EDMUND HUSSERL translated by W. R. BOYCE GIBSON
Identity and Reality by EMILE MEYERSON

Muirhead Library of Philosophy

EDITED BY H. D. LEWIS

ETHICAL KNOWLEDGE

ETHICAL
KNOWLEDGE

By

JOEL J. KUPPERMAN

*Associate Professor of Philosophy
at the University of Connecticut*

LONDON · GEORGE ALLEN & UNWIN LTD
NEW YORK · HUMANITIES PRESS INC.

PRINTED IN GREAT BRITAIN
in 11 point Imprint type
BY W & J MACKAY & CO, LTD, CHATHAM

PREFACE

The philosophical problem addressed by this book is perhaps the one most relevant to the life of the average unphilosophical man. It can be argued that every man assumes a solution in his life. It may be so deeply assumed that it never is questioned, thought about, or even articulated. It may be the result of childhood training, or conversely of an almost instinctive distrust of conventional wisdom, or the result of various other influences separate from philosophy. Any problem that is this important deserves repeated philosophical examination.

The reader who expects to find here a highly 'existential' treatment of ethical knowledge will be disappointed. Such a treatment can have great value, but only after analytical work at the foundations has been done. Much of the first half of this book is historical or exploratory. The second half is highly analytical, examining the relations between ethical claims and other kinds of claims that generally are accorded cognitive status. This is designed to be work of a kind with which advanced students in philosophy are most familiar. But the book would not have been written had I not believed that it could have uses which were more than academic.

I am greatly indebted to Karen, Michael, and Charles Kupperman, my wife and sons, whose cheerfulness has sustained me. A number of colleagues and former colleagues have helped me philosophically: I wish especially to thank Ruth Millikan, D. H. Rice, and Jerome Shaffer.

CONTENTS

PART I

BACKGROUNDS AND
PRELIMINARY OBSERVATIONS

CHAPTER I

THE NATURE OF THE PROBLEM

Is there ethical knowledge? I shall argue that there is. Before the argument begins, though, three things must be settled. We must decide what it is that the argument is intended to establish (what 'ethical knowledge' is); we must decide also what methods and arguments are relevant; and we must also have arrived at a clear picture of what some major recent philosophers have said about the question, and of what might be called the climate of intellectual opinion. The latter task is assayed in the next four chapters. In this chapter I shall clarify the question, and the techniques which I shall use.

A major part of my work here is to avoid confusion and oversimplification. Questions closely related to 'Is there ethical knowledge?' have suffered a great deal in this century, as we shall see, from over-simple approaches. One point which will emerge is that 'Is there ethical knowledge?' is not the kind of question which can be answered by means of the straightforward application of one or two simple criteria, nor one which can be answered merely by means of the luminous character of a few well-chosen examples. It is not to be confused with questions which can be answered in this way.

One confusion which should be ruled out immediately is that between 'ethical knowledge' and 'knowledge in ethics'. It is clear that at least some knowledge is contained in ethics. It is clear, for example, that ethical statements usually convey knowledge of the attitudes of the person who makes them. If someone says 'Violence is bad', we normally know that he disapproves of violence. Ethical statements also may embody, or convey, knowledge of what the consequences of an action may be expected to be ('You really ought not to push that button'), or of what the mores or laws of society are ('You ought to stop at that stop sign'). Thus if the question is 'Is there knowledge in ethics?' we can answer 'Yes' now, and end our discussion.

Indeed, virtually no philosopher has denied that there is knowledge in ethics. A. J. Ayer, for example, who is often thought of as an arch 'non-cognitivist' in ethics, says that ethical works typically contain 'propositions which express definitions of ethical terms', and also 'propositions which describe the phenomena of moral experience, and their causes', which 'must be assigned to the science of psychology, or sociology'.[1] Given Ayer's respect for logic and the sciences of psychology and sociology, we can see that this is tantamount to recognizing that there is something of the 'cognitive' in ethics. Stevenson speaks of ethics as having 'cognitive aspects'; and by these it is clear that he means not only that beliefs, and reasons relating to beliefs, are relevant to disagreements in attitudes, but also that an ethical statement normally embodies (self) knowledge as to what the speaker approves or disapproves of.[2]

Thus 'Is there knowledge in ethics?' is an easy question, and does not capture any of the outlines of the issue about the status of ethics which has been so much debated in this century. As we shall see, the question 'Is there ethical knowledge?' does capture some of the outlines of this issue.

The issue has sometimes been formulated as 'Is ethics (or morals) cognitive?' It has been formulated this way mainly by philosophers who wished to take the affirmative side.[3] It ought to be clear that this is a misleading formulation. One of its weaknesses is that philosophers who are to be assigned to the negative side of the debate are in fact unwilling to answer unequivocally 'No'. As we have seen, Ayer and Stevenson do believe that ethics has 'cognitive' aspects.

It is extremely difficult however to define adequately what it is which I (and other people who have argued unequivocally that

---

[1] A. J. Ayer, *Language Truth and Logic* (New York: Dover Publications, 1947), p. 103.

[2] *Ethics and Language* (New Haven: Yale University Press, 1960), p. 23.

[3] See for example Philip Blair Rice, 'Ethical Empiricism and Its Critics', *Philosophical Review*, Vol. LXII (1953), p. 373; K. Kolenda, 'Science and Morality', *Mind*, Vol. LXVII, (1958); Peter Glassen, 'The Cognitivity of Moral Judgments', *Mind*, Vol. LXVIII (1959); and Alan Gewirth, 'Positive "Ethics" and Normative "Science" ', *Philosophical Review*, Vol. LXIX (1960). Gewirth does not himself put forward a 'cognitivist' position, but merely is concerned to argue against some objections to 'cognitivist' positions. A number of other philosophers have formulated what (in the hands of most of them) appears to be essentially the same issue as that of 'Is ethics (or morals) objective (or has it objectivity)?' See for example H. Sidgwick, *Methods of Ethics* (London: Macmillan & Co., 1893), pp. 27ff.; A. C. Ewing, *The Definition of Good* (New York: Macmillan, 1947), Chapter 1; A. C. Ewing, *Ethics* (New York: Collier Books, 1962), pp. 107ff.; William Kneale, 'Objectivity in Morals', *Philosophy*, Vol. XXV (1950); John Rawls, 'Outline of a Decision Procedure for Ethics', *Philosophical Review*, Vol. LX (1951), p. 177; Bernard Mayo, *Ethics and the Moral Life* (London: Macmillan & Co., 1958), pp. 69ff.; and Carl Wellman, 'Emotivism and Ethical Objectivity', *American Philosophical Quarterly*, Vol. 5 (1968). It is clear that the thesis for which Sidgwick, Ewing, and Mayo wish to argue, is closely similar to the thesis of this book. I am inclined to think that Rawls and Wellman are addressing pretty much this issue, but that Kneale is not.

ethics is 'cognitive', as well as most of the philosophers who have argued that ethics is 'objective') wish to maintain and which Ayer and Stevenson would not accept. A first attempt might run as follows. The knowledge which Ayer and Stevenson perceive within ethics all belongs to psychology, sociology, the natural sciences, or to logic. Let us define ethical knowledge as knowledge contained in ethics which does *not* belong to psychology, sociology, the natural sciences, or to logic. Given this formulation, we see that Ayer and Stevenson both maintained that there is no ethical knowledge; it also would appear that most of the philosophers who were most anxious to argue that ethics is 'cognitive' or 'objective' were saying, or were willing to say, that there is ethical knowledge.

This will do as a first approach. It does explain why I much prefer to ask 'Is there ethical knowledge?' to asking 'Is ethics cognitive?' One difficulty, though, is that the definition just given of ethical knowledge was entirely negative. I merely characterized it as knowledge which did not fit into various established categories.

One might be tempted to define ethical knowledge positively as knowledge of right and wrong, what we are obligated to do, and of values. The major difficulty here is that the definition is harmful if it is construed as saying that ethical knowledge is *about* right and wrong, obligations, and values; and if it further leads one to consider the reality of that which ethical knowledge is about. It sounds very implausible to say that ethical knowledge is *about* anything, in the sense in which psychological or chemical knowledge is about something. G. E. Moore talked rather this way in *Principia Ethica*, but it is important to stipulate that belief in ethical knowledge does not commit one to any ontological superstructure. I shall discuss this further in Chapter II.

With the stipulation that it does not involve any ontological commitment, the preceding definition of ethical knowledge (as knowledge of right and wrong, what we are obligated to do, and of values) is a helpful introductory definition. It becomes more useful if it is supplemented by examples. Here are three examples of cases in which I shall argue that there is ethical knowledge.

1. A has been told that murder is wrong. He and Z are in love with the same woman. A has a splendid opportunity to murder Z, with every chance of not being detected; but he restrains himself, saying, 'This would be immoral.' (A knows that it would be wrong to kill Z.)

2. B is the landlord of a very poor family. He has an opportunity to increase his profit by evicting them, and then raising the rent on the apartment that they have occupied. However, B has reflected that the attempt to promote human happiness is at the foundations of ethics; he knows that his evicting the poor family will produce on balance more unhappiness than happiness; and he thus concludes that he ought not to evict them, and accordingly restrains himself. (B knows that he ought not to evict his poor tenants.)

3. C craves pleasure. Thanks to a timely inheritance, he has the opportunity to pursue for several years a life directed entirely towards his own pleasure. He finds this subtly unsatisfactory, and tries instead then to lead a life which centres on commitments and purposes which he shares with other people. He finds this manner of life much more satisfactory. (C knows that a life directed entirely towards one's own pleasure is less satisfactory than a life which centres on commitments and purposes which are shared with others.)

Ayer and Stevenson would recognize, of course, that there is knowledge of some kind related to, or embodied in, the ethical judgments of A, B, and C. My position is that knowledge over and above scientific or logical knowledge is embodied in their judgments. To put the point more specifically, my position is that A has knowledge over and above both the psychological knowledge of his own attitudes and the sociological knowledge that in our society murder is considered wrong; one might say that he knows that murder really is wrong. B has more than the sociological knowledge of society's reaction to his actions, or the psychological knowledge of his own attitudes, or the logical knowledge of the implications of a utilitarian-like position; he knows that evicting the poor family really would be wrong. C also knows more than how he and others feel; he knows that a life directed entirely towards one's own pleasure really is inadequate.

My distinction between psychological and sociological knowledge on one hand, and ethical knowledge on the other, can be made more clear if we consider the following hypothetical case. We ask A, 'If you, and everyone else in the world (including ourselves), had been given a pill such that its taker came to consider killing a rival perfectly desirable in cases involving passion, would killing a rival in such a case then be right?' Now my position is that if A's knowledge that killing Z is wrong were purely psychological or sociological, and if he realized this, then his recognition that, after the pill, everyone would have pro-attitudes towards passionate killing of rivals, should make him judge that killing Z would not be wrong. In fact A is likely not to judge this; furthermore, if he did judge that, after the pill, killing Z would not be wrong, we would be likely to say that his previous knowledge had not been that killing Z was wrong, but rather that killing Z was considered wrong. (In a legal sense, of course, he still would be said to have known that killing his rival is wrong. I shall discuss this in Chapter VIII.)

In order to avoid misunderstanding, I should stress that this example is not being put forward as an argument against Stevenson or Ayer. (Arguments will come in the third and fourth chapters; right now we are working on distinctions.) It is clear that a follower of Stevenson's indeed would have his own account of the pill case. He probably would say that, even if A's post-pill attitude towards killing Z would hypothetically have been favourable, the attitude that A actually has now, is what is expressed (or, in Stevenson's early account, described) in his judgment that it would be wrong to kill Z. Thus it can be argued, with considerable plausibility, that Stevenson can account for the pill case as well as I can; and at this point in the book I am not yet ready to argue against this.

My point for the time being is simply this. If A insists that he knows that killing Z would be wrong even if he and everyone else had a favourable attitude towards killing a rival, and if he construes his judgment as not being simply a description of his own present attitude, this shows that he conceives of his knowledge that killing Z is wrong as not being psychological or sociological knowledge. Stevenson and Ayer in effect would have to say that A, in claiming that he has knowledge here which is not psychological or sociological (or belonging to logic or the natural sciences) is suffering from a philosophical illusion. Whether A is suffering from an illusion or not will be argued later in the book. For the time being, I shall entertain the notion that he is not, to the extent of accepting his implicit distinction between ethical knowledge on one hand, and psychological or sociological knowledge on the other.

If we apply the pill hypothesis to the cases of B and C, we get somewhat contrasting results. B's knowledge can be treated very similarly to A's knowledge. C's knowledge that a life directed entirely towards one's own pleasure is not entirely satisfactory, on the other hand, might seem to pose special problems, since a psychological reaction appears especially crucial to it. We might however ask C whether he would want a life which contained all of the experiences which he had when he was entirely concerned with own pleasure, with the one exception that he was satisfied with such a life. (This is a little like asking 'Would you like to be a satisfied pig?' or the question which Socrates poses in the *Philebus*, 'Would you like to be a titillated oyster, with as good a memory or intellect as an oyster normally has?') Now if C's judgment had been an ethical judgment, rather than a personal, psychological judgment, it implied that other people who led lives directed entirely towards their own pleasure were leading unsatisfactory lives, even if they themselves did not feel so. Therefore C would have to answer 'No'. In terms of my distinction, an answer of 'No' shows that C's knowledge, while it had been intimately related to (psychological) self-knowledge, was ethical knowledge.

Having said this, I should add that the line between ethical knowledge and psychological knowledge is far more blurred in cases like C's than in cases like A's and B's. A related issue is that of whether psychology (or for that matter sociology or history) can be, or should be, 'value-free'. If one answers in the affirmative, then the line between psychological, sociological, and historical knowledge on one side, and ethical knowledge on the other, becomes sharp. If one answers in the negative, then it is possible to produce cases which are very much on the borderline between ethical and psychological, sociological, or historical knowledge. The case of C arguably would be very close to the borderline. C's knowledge, if it is that lives directed entirely towards one's own pleasure are unsatisfactory even on the part of people who like such lives, is ethical knowledge; yet the evidence for it is going to be very largely psychological, and it might naturally find a place in a value-ridden account of the psychology of pleasure-seeking. (This consideration may help us to appreciate the relevance of 'Know thyself' to ethics, and to appreciate also the major role which psychological observations have played in so many ethical treatises.)

Let us return to explicating the problem of ethical knowledge. It is time to admit three major difficulties in my account of what I shall be arguing to exist, i.e. of what ethical knowledge, if there is such a thing, is. One is the difficulty of giving a better than broad definition of ethical knowledge. This difficulty appears to exist for most branches of knowledge. The definition 'Ethical knowledge is knowledge of right and wrong, of what we are obligated to do, and of values' is broad, but so are the definitions of psychological and sociological knowledge at the beginnings of psychology and sociology textbooks. It is assumed that, as one gets into the subject matter, the bare bones of the definition will take on flesh. The student has a better idea of what psychology or sociology is, after he has studied it for a while. In the same way, I might presume on the reader's familiarity with problems of ethics.

If, however, one attempts to supplement a broad definition by means of specific examples, there is a second difficulty. One encounters cases which are on, or close to, a borderline with another subject. For example, the nature of psychological knowledge might be illustrated by, among other examples, knowledge of how someone relates his attitudes to the dominant attitudes of the group to which he belongs. This is very close, however, to the borderline with sociology. In the same way, C's knowledge is arguably very close to the borderline between ethics and psychology. Presumably, again, someone who is familiar with a subject can cope with, or adjust to the idea of, borderline cases.

A third major difficulty is this: I have said that in this chapter I am making distinctions, rather than producing arguments; but in philosophy, distinctions are almost always tendentious, and may subtly blend into arguments. Clearly a so-called 'non-cognitivist' would not be entirely happy with everything that I have said thus far. On the other hand, a philosopher who made only philosophically neutral remarks on the subject of ethical knowledge would be restricted to vapid and unfruitful commonplaces. Let me claim this much for my distinctions. I have not assumed too much; the deck has not been stacked. The best evidence for this is the difficulty of the remaining chapters. Even with the groundwork of my distinctions, the argument that there is ethical knowledge, is not going to come very easily.

This much may be added. What I have said thus far has been directed primarily towards a classification of ethics as distinct from other disciplines, or rather towards a distinction between those elements in ethics which are irreducibly ethical and those elements which may be assigned to other disciplines. In this respect Ayer at least might not be too thoroughly upset by the outlines of my distinctions. He in fact takes pains to distinguish the elements in ethical works which are psychological or sociological (and therefore cognitive) from the normative elements (which according to him are not cognitive). The issue between 'non-cognitivists' and me does not appear to be primarily one of classification (although secondarily it may involve some differences in classification).

The primary issue rather appears to be this: given some classification which does not consider ethics to be entirely analysable, without residue, into psychology, sociology, etc., do we say that statements pertaining to ethics may embody or convey knowledge which cannot be immediately assigned to psychology, sociology, etc.? This clearly is a point at which Ayer and Stevenson want to say 'No', and I wish to say 'Yes'. But what precisely is at issue here?

The issue often has been put in terms of truth.[1] In the example of A, those who argued that ethics is 'cognitive' have usually wanted in effect to say that A's statement ('It would be wrong to kill Z') is true, and furthermore that its truth is not merely a matter of whether it mirrors A's attitude or not, or of whether we agree with it or not. Thus the issue of whether ethics is 'cognitive' has been made to hang on the claim that ethical statements may be true.

Actually the issues here are extremely complicated. Stevenson has been willing to speak of ethical statements, in one or two senses, as being true. Clearly he has not been willing to speak of them as true in the sense in which 'cognitivists' wish to speak of them as true, but the differences are subtle. I shall discuss this in Chapter III. By that point, however, I also shall have developed an argument against putting the issue at all in terms of truth. I shall argue in Chapter II that, in most concrete cases, 'right' and 'correct' are more natural words than 'true' to use in connection with ethical claims. This is not a minor point: it means that a writer like Moore, who wishes consistently to use 'true' in connection with ethical claims, is forced as a result to give an extremely artificial picture of ethics, which in turn discredits the view that there is ethical knowledge.

For the time being, let us formulate the issue of ethical knowledge in terms of the correctness of judgments. We may distinguish between judgments which are correct in an unqualified sense, and judgments which are correct in a qualified sense. The correctness of judgments which are correct in an unqualified sense is independent of (not simply a function of) the attitude or opinion of the person making them, the agreement of the person responding to them, or the opinion of society. The correctness of judgments

---

[1] Ewing, for example, speaks of the issue of whether ethical judgments have 'what is called a cognitive function, i.e. whether they also make assertions which can be called true or false'. (*Ethics*, p. 107.)

which are correct in a qualified sense is dependent on (that is, a function of) the attitude or opinion of the person making them, the agreement of the person responding to them, or the opinion of society. In terms of this distinction, we may say that to claim that there is ethical knowledge implies the claim that ethical judgments may be correct in an unqualified sense. Anyone who denies that ethical judgments may be correct in an unqualified sense thereby denies that there is ethical knowledge. (Pretty clearly those writers who have denied that ethical statements are true in what I have called 'an unqualified sense' would also deny that ethical judgments may be correct in an unqualified sense.) It follows from this that anyone who regards the correctness of ethical judgments as obtaining simply in virtue of their correctly describing (or adequately expressing) the attitudes of the person making them thereby denies that there is ethical knowledge. Anyone who regards the correctness of ethical judgments as obtaining simply in terms of the agreement in attitude of the person who hears the statements thereby denies that there is ethical knowledge. Anyone who regards the correctness of ethical judgments as obtaining simply in terms of the agreement of these judgments with social norms thereby denies that there is ethical knowledge. Finally, anyone who simply denies that ethical judgments can be correct thereby denies that there is ethical knowledge.

Plainly there has to be a little more to the affirmative side than just the assertion that some ethical judgments are correct in an unqualified sense. After all, one can speak the truth without having knowledge, and one can do something correctly without having knowledge. Yet some recent 'cognitivists' have not gone much beyond discussing the truth of ethical statements.

It might be argued, indeed, that the thesis which I shall argue in this book is stronger, and therefore more questionable, than the thesis which most recent 'cognitivists' and 'objectivists' have had in mind. But, in rebuttal, at least as regards the 'cognitivists', it should be pointed out that the word 'cognitive' is very closely related in meaning to 'knowledge'. If a philosopher believed in ethical truth but not in ethical knowledge, it would be extremely clumsy of him to formulate his view as the view that ethics is 'cognitive'. Furthermore there have been good reasons for a 'cognitivist' to spend his time discussing the truth of ethical statements, to the neglect of other factors related to ethical knowledge: the unqualified truth of ethical statements has been the most debatable point. Thus it seems likely that most recent 'cognitivists' would agree with me that there is ethical knowledge, and I suspect that most recent 'objectivists' would also.

How do we establish that there is ethical knowledge? Clearly a part of the argument will have to be that there are ethical judgments which are unqualifiedly correct. But how do we establish this?

The obvious, and modish, answer is to rely on an examination of ordinary language. Do we, and how do we, use words like 'true', 'right' and 'correct' in relation to ethical statements and judgments?

There are three major difficulties here. One is that the issue is, after all, not whether we use 'true', 'right' and 'correct', but whether we use them in a certain way. Now it is clear that 'true', 'right' and 'correct' often are used in connection with ethical claims. But a 'non-cognitivist' writer such as Stevenson can point this out, without compromising his position. He simply can interpret the uses of 'true' in ethics (those, at least, which he regards as not 'confused') as what we have called 'qualified'. I shall argue that what we might call 'common sense interpretations' of ordinary language are themselves part of ordinary language, and support a 'cognitivist' position; but the fact remains that a straightforward check of what might be called 'the surface facts' of ordinary language is not enough to refute, or to validate Stevenson's account, simply because Stevenson has his own interpretation of these data.

This is tied to a second difficulty. Stevenson's and Ayer's work on ethics was heavily dependent on logical positivist theories of meaning. Even if one argues that the uses of 'true', 'right' and 'correct' in ordinary ethical discourse must be interpreted as unqualified, this does not constitute final refutation of Stevenson. Stevenson then can argue that ordinary language in this area is confused (perhaps by the influence of his philosophical predecessors), or can argue simply that there are overriding philosophical reasons for his account. As we shall see, Stevenson did make remarks of this character. Thus an argument that the weight of ordinary discourse is against Stevenson and Ayer does not settle the matter. In order to settle it we have, at the very least, to descend (or ascend) to the level of philosophical theory, and to argue against logical positivism. (This argument itself may involve an appeal to ordinary language, but as it were to much larger and more fundamental structures of ordinary language.)

A third difficulty in relying too heavily on the occurrence of words like 'correct' in ordinary speech about ethical judgments is this. Dominant patterns in ordinary language are subject to change. In Chapter V, I shall point out how the popular influence of relativist positions indicates the possibility of change in the most common patterns of ethical discourse. Even if it is argued that ordinary language today is predominantly 'cognitivist', it might also be argued that it should not be; and it might also be argued that in fifty, or a hundred, years ordinary language will be predominantly 'non-cognitivist'.

Thus an argument that ethical judgments may be unqualifiedly correct because this is implicit in most of our ordinary ethical discourse, is not entirely conclusive. A philosopher who argues this way may be assailed as incorrigibly conservative in his assumptions. 'Why should we continue to accept the patterns of current ordinary language?', it may be asked. Some people may feel, indeed, that precisely one of the tasks of philosophy is to improve, or to eliminate 'confusions' within, the structure of ordinary language.

Let me add the following comments. First, even if the patterns of ordinary language need not be accepted as beyond appeal, the burden of argument is always on the man who wishes to modify ordinary language. If indeed the most common forms of ethical discourse in which we ordinarily engage imply that ethical judgments may be unqualifiedly correct, then we must perforce believe that ethical judgments may be unqualifiedly correct, unless there are overriding reasons against this.

Secondly, the overriding reasons may be of two characters. They may be philosophical. For example, it might be argued on the basis of a logical positivist theory of meaning that ordinary ethical discourse tends to include key phrases or assertions whose meanings are confused. Or the overriding reasons may themselves be ethical. For example, it might be argued that the most common patterns of our ethical discourse promote intolerance, and are therefore undesirable. As I shall point out in the fifth chapter, much of the appeal of popular relativism is based on explicit or implicit arguments of this latter character.

Thus, in order to argue that ethical judgments may be unqualifiedly correct, I shall have to develop arguments of three characters. I shall argue that the most common patterns of ordinary ethical discourse must be interpreted as implying that ethical judgments may be unqualifiedly correct. I also shall argue, defensively, that there are no compelling ethical reasons for preferring a pattern of ethical discourse which does not imply that ethical judgments may be unqualifiedly correct. Finally, I also shall have to argue, defensively, that there are no overriding philosophical reasons for denying that ethical judgments may be unqualifiedly correct, i.e. I shall argue against the logical positivist critique of ethics.

The larger argument that there is ethical knowledge will have components of these three characters. It is worth mentioning that a part of the third component—which involves a defence against philosophical objections—will be somewhat reminiscent of legal argument. The defence against the charge that there is no ethical knowledge will rest in part on similarities of the case at hand to precedent cases. Ethical 'knowledge', I shall argue, has important similarities to generally recognized examples of knowledge, and thus so to speak is 'innocent'. The attempt to discuss similarities and differences between what purports to be ethical 'knowledge', on one hand, and other forms of 'knowledge' on the other, will provide one of the themes of this book.

CHAPTER II

G. E. MOORE'S *PRINCIPIA ETHICA*

Moore clearly held a position which came close to affirming that there is ethical knowledge. He almost certainly would have agreed, at least when he wrote *Principia Ethica* (and for some decades beyond), that there is ethical knowledge. In the Preface to *Principia Ethica*, he speaks of his book as a 'Prologomena to any future Ethics that can possibly pretend to be scientific'.[1] In Chapter IV he remarks that 'It is said, with sufficient truth, that you would never know a thing was good unless you preferred it . . .'.[2] Throughout *Principia Ethica* he speaks of ethical statements as true and false.[3]

Thus *Principia Ethica* is clearly on the affirmative side of the debate in this century over whether ethics is 'cognitive'. We may go further than this. *Principia Ethica* was published first in 1903, at a time when the debate had not really taken form; it was, and is, an impressive and influential book. We may say, then, that for a long time the affirmative side of the debate was closely identified with *Principia Ethica*. For a long time, that is, philosophers tended to associate the view that ethics is 'cognitive' with the general position of *Principia Ethica*. This undoubtedly has been far less true since World War II than it had been previously; but Moore's ethics retains some influence, including influence over the way some philosophers view the problems of this book.

This influence is in many respects unfortunate. Moore presented the 'cognitivist' position in conjunction with some extremely vulnerable doctrines in what might be called the ontology and epistemology of ethics. Critics who have attacked these doctrines have believed that their attacks refuted also the general 'cognitivist' position.

As a result it is highly necessary for me, despite my admiration for Moore, to disassociate the position of this book from that of *Principia Ethica*. This amounts to showing that one can argue the 'cognitivist' position differently. A large part of this will involve

---

[1] *Principia Ethica* (Cambridge: Cambridge University Press, 1954), p. ix.
[2] *ibid.* p. 132.
[3] *ibid.*, pp. viii, ix, 1, 21, 23, 27, 44, 193, 207; *The Philosophy of G. E. Moore*, ed. Schilpp (New York: Tudor, 1952), p. 544.

pointing out assumptions which Moore made in *Principia Ethica*, and which appear both untenable and unnecessary.

The two most obvious questions which will be put to a philosopher who believes that there is ethical knowledge, or who holds some similar or approximate view, are (1) 'If there is ethical knowledge, how do we acquire it?', and (2) 'If there is ethical knowledge, what is it about?' Moore in effect answered both of these questions. We shall examine the way in which he answered them, and the disastrous effect it had on his position.

I

According to Moore, we can legitimately arrive at judgments of intrinsic value only be means of 'intuition'. For example, the question of whether virtuous actions and dispositions are good in themselves 'must be settled by intuition alone'.[1] We may, and should, arrive at judgments of what ought to be done by means of a more complicated process. This includes both calculating the probabilities that the choices open to us will have various consequences, and weighing intuitions of the values of these consequences.

Moore's use of 'intuition' presents problems. Because of it, Moore is often called an 'intuitionist' (despite his attempt to reserve this label for philosophers who consider rules of action self-evident). The label is one which most ethical philosophers nowadays would be anxious to avoid. 'Intuition' suggests arcane mental processes. On the other hand, Moore's defenders argue that the word merely is intended to make a logical point, and that in *Principia Ethica* it does not describe any special psychological process.

It is certain that Moore *intended* the word 'intuition' to make a logical rather than a psychological point. He says in the Preface that '. . . when I call such propositions "Intuitions", I mean *merely* to assert that they are incapable of proof; I imply nothing whatever as to the manner or origin of our cognition of them.'[2] Thus the text does seem to bear out the view of Moore's defenders. But there is a major difficulty. This is in separating the logical point from the psychological point. To say that intuitions are incapable of proof necessarily *is* to imply something as to 'the manner or origin of our cognition of them'. It implies that when intuitions are arrived at intelligently, they are not the result of accepting a proof. This is

---

[1] *Principia Ethica*, p. 173.   [2] *ibid.*, p. x; italics are Moore's.

both a logical and a psychological point, and it is hard to see how its two aspects can be separated.

The logical point that Moore primarily wished to make has a great deal to do with Moore's rejection of the naturalistic fallacy. Indeed this (from Moore's point of view) is the central matter of *Principia Ethica*. As Moore described it, the naturalistic fallacy is the fallacy of identifying goodness with some natural property. To commit the naturalistic fallacy is to claim that one can construct valid deductive proofs in which the premises merely describe natural properties and the conclusion is about goodness. Moore argued that in fact no description of natural properties ever logically commits one to an ethical judgment: the ethical questions remain 'open questions'.

Moore's opposition to the naturalistic fallacy was extreme. I may say that I accept what might be called a 'minimal' form of Moore's view concerning the naturalistic fallacy. That is, I agree that it is impossible to construct valid deductive proofs in which the premises merely describe natural properties and the conclusion is about goodness.[1] However, unfortunately, Moore said much more than this. It appears that he was influenced by a formal logic in which no logical support weaker than implication was recognized. He seemed to feel that there were only two alternatives: either judgments of intrinsic value could be deduced from descriptions of natural properties or there was no logical relation at all. Thus Moore says not only that judgments of intrinsic value cannot be deduced from descriptions of natural properties: he says that 'no relevant evidence can be adduced' to support judgments of intrinsic value.[2]

This is plainly false. If someone says 'X has given very amply and inconspicuously to the poor, behaves lovingly to his family, and has not broken any of the traditionally recognized moral laws: therefore he is a good man, and has many good states of mind', we are all inclined to regard this as reasonable. We are all inclined to regard the descriptions of X's activities as lending some logical weight to a favourable evaluation of X's states of mind, although it does not constitute a valid deductive argument. As many writers have pointed out, we do reason about values; and it is paradoxical

[1] For an especially ingenious attempt, cf. John Searle, 'How to Derive "Ought" from "Is"', *Philosophical Review*, Vol. LXXIII (1964). For rebuttal, cf. James Thomson and Judith Thomson, 'How Not to Derive "Ought" From "Is"', *Philosophical Review*, Vol. LXXIII (1964); also Jan F. Narveson, *Morality and Utility* (Baltimore: Johns Hopkins Press, 1967), pp. 189–92.

[2] *Principia Ethica*, p. viii.

to maintain, as Moore and Stevenson both did, that the reasons have at most a psychological relation to our value judgments.[1]

Part of the burden of Moore's word 'intuition', is then that Moore excludes all reasoning from what he calls 'intuition'. He also perforce excludes what we normally call perception, or sensory experience, since goodness is not a natural quality. What is left? Logically we are left with the view that judgments of intrinsic value are 'self-evident'.[2] We are also left with a picture of the convinced follower of Moore's, arriving at a value judgment: he does not reason as a way of arriving at it, and he does not rely on his senses. One is tempted to imagine him closing his eyes, and coming up with an answer. It is this sort of thing that has given 'intuitionism' a bad name.

The word 'intuition' in Moore's use carries the suggestion that we cannot provide rational support for judgments of what is in itself valuable. But this runs counter to fact.[3] Thus Moore's use of 'intuition' is misleading.

My own view is this. It is important to avoid any locution which suggests that there are simple answers to the question 'How do we acquire ethical knowledge?' The proper answer is extremely complex. As I shall show in Chapters VI and VII, reason and experience both are often involved in the acquisition of ethical knowledge: the degree and nature of the involvement varies with the kind of case, and in my view no recent writer has done anything like justice to the complexity of this. Moore's view of how we acquire knowledge of values looks far too simple. It looks too simple for two reasons especially. One is that Moore's view of the logical relation between facts and judgments of intrinsic value is too simple. The other is Moore's unwise use of the word 'intuition'.

II

The question, 'What is ethical knowledge about?', if it is interpreted as asking for an object of ethical knowledge, is one which in my opinion should not be given even a complex answer. The question reflects unwarranted assumptions. Moore did, however, answer

[1] For an admirable discussion of this, with which I concur, see George Kerner, *The Revolution in Ethical Theory* (Oxford: Oxford University Press, 1966), pp. 32–5.

[2] *Principia Ethica*, p. 143.

[3] For historical examples of such rational support see Aristotle's arguments that the contemplative life is in itself valuable, or Mill's argument that the 'higher pleasures' are intrinsically more valuable than the 'lower pleasures'.

this question very simply. His answer did a great deal to introduce extraneous issues into discussions of the 'cognitive' character of ethics.

According to Moore, propositions about what is intrinsically good are about the non-natural quality of goodness. This quality has a peculiar ontological status. Moore speaks of the class of objects which 'do not *exist* at all. To this class, as I have said, belongs what we mean by the adjective "good". . . . The most prominent members of this class are perhaps numbers. . . . Two *is* somehow, although it does not exist.'[1] Thus Moore's ethical theory, at least at the time when he wrote *Principia Ethica*, involves the view that there is ethical being.

Moore arrived at this view apparently from two directions. On one hand he wanted to credit ethical propositions with meaning, and felt that in order for ethical terms to have meaning they had to correspond to something. Moore's theory of meaning, whether it was an 'object theory' or as Alan White thinks a 'concept theory', was a 'naming theory'.[2] It called for ethical realities corresponding to ethical language.

On the other hand, Moore also was encouraged to posit ethical entities by his theory of truth. As I have remarked, Moore believed that ethical propositions are true or false. White speaks of the mistaken assumption of a correspondence theory of truth, which his other writings show Moore made . . .'.[3] Presumably, then, true ethical propositions correspond to something in reality: this again might make it seem reasonable to suppose that there are non-natural ethical qualities which have 'being'.

But to speak this way seems excessively metaphysical, as it does to distinguish between 'being' and 'existence'. Also Moore, when he posits the being of ethical qualities, is vulnerable to Occam's Razor. It is impossible to exaggerate the extent to which this aspect of Moore's theory not only has influenced the form of consideration of the 'cognitivist' view, but also has discredited that view.

Certainly this weakness in *Principia Ethica* has been widely noted in recent years. Stephen Toulmin, for example, remarks,

'There is no reason in the world why all of our words should act as names for definite and unique processes—physical or mental: only

---

[1] *Principia Ethica*, pp. 110–11; italics are Moore's.
[2] Alan R. White, *G. E. Moore, A Critical Exposition* (Oxford: Basil Blackwell, 1959), pp. 40–1.
[3] *ibid.*, p. 138.

some of them, in fact are of such a kind that it makes sense to talk of such processes. And we can easily see that the class of concepts for which it does make sense cannot include ethical concepts.'[1]

The question 'What is ethical knowledge about?' is illegitimate for the following reason. There is no strict logical requirement that knowledge be *about* anything, in the sense of having an object which possesses being. Many philosophers would want to say that there is mathematical knowledge but that numbers do not have being. As Toulmin suggests, it is especially plausible to talk of ethical concepts as not having objects.

Moore's error here, in my opinion, is at a deeper level than just his ethical ontology. Indeed we might ask, 'How much do we peel away in order to make Moore's view plausible?' Certainly the view that there is ethical truth and that ethics is 'cognitive' can stand without the preposterous ontology of *Principia Ethica* or the theory of meaning which engendered it. We also could do without the correspondence theory of truth in relation to ethics. Again the example of mathematics is useful in convincing us that a specious requirement is not universal: most philosophers would concede that some mathematical propositions are true, and virtually no one would apply the correspondence theory of truth to mathematics.[2] (This is not to suggest that there is any anlogy between ethics and mathematics. The argument is simply that a requirement which does not extend to mathematical knowledge is not a universal requirement, therefore may have other exceptions, and therefore need not be assumed to apply to ethical knowledge.)

I suggest that we peel away one more layer from Moore's view here. It is not at all obvious that in order for ethics to be 'cognitive' there has to be ethical truth. After all, we do normally speak of people as 'knowing' how to ride a bicycle, even though there is no common tendency to applaud good performances at bicycle riding as 'true'. Furthermore, I shall argue, the word 'true' can be used systematically in connection with ethical statements only at the cost of considerable distortion.

---

[1] *The Place of Reason in Ethics* (Cambridge: Cambridge University Press, 1961), p. 44.

[2] John Austin did, however, suggest that it is inappropriate to speak of arithmetical formulas or geometrical axioms as 'true'. Cf. John Austin, 'Truth', *Truth*, ed. George Pitcher (Englewood Cliffs, New Jersey: Prentice Hall, 1964), pp. 29–30. As the reader will see, I shall endorse, or rather describe, a somewhat similar move with regard to ethics. My point above is that one could speak of ethical claims as 'true' without thereby making any ontological commitments.

In order to see this we have to look at the word 'true' and its relatives. Examples of these are 'right' and 'correct'. The spheres in which these words and 'true' are ordinarily used overlap. If we ask someone 'What is the capital of Connecticut?', and he answers 'Hartford', we may say 'True', 'Right' or 'Correct'; although if the incident firmly has the character of question-and-answer we would be more likely to use one of the latter two words, especially 'correct'. (In general we may be slightly more prone to speak of acceptable performance of a practical task as 'right' than as 'correct', especially when the alternatives are not sharply delineated: we speak of the right way of riding a bicycle, but also of the correct order of steps in assembling an amplifier.) Most of the distinctions which can be drawn between 'right' and 'correct' do not concern us here. Instead we are concerned to draw a distinction between 'true' and its relatives.

The most basic distinction appears to be this. 'True' is most naturally used in connection with mathematical and factual propositions, treated in relative isolation both from other propositions and from performances, such as the performance of arriving at them. Thus we speak normally of propositions in an arithmatic text as true; we say 'It is true that it rained yesterday'; and we speak of the allegations of a journalist or a historian as true. 'It rained yesterday' however is not a 'true answer' to the question 'What was the weather like yesterday?': it is rather a 'correct' or 'right' answer. There also are not true descriptions.[1] Collections of propositions which are intimately interrelated in meaning or import, or propositions which are closely tied to a theoretical base, tend also not to be spoken of as 'true' or 'false'. Gibbon's history is not 'true': it is more or less 'accurate' or 'faithful'. Einstein's theory may be spoken of as 'true', but it more commonly would be spoken of as 'acceptable' or 'good'.

It is possible to speak without excessive oddity of ethical statements as 'true', but only under two conditions. First, one must treat the statements abstractly: that is, out of the context of relations to performances. (It is possible to say 'It is true that parents ought to punish misbehaving children'; but when a parent says 'I have decided that parents ought to punish misbehaving children', we are much more likely to say 'I think you are right' than 'True'.) Secondly, one must treat the statements out of the context of any

[1] Cf. S. E. Toulmin and K. Baier, 'On Describing', *Mind*, Vol. LXI (1952).

intimate relations of meaning with other statements or with underlying theories. (We may say 'It is true that a life free from pain is
desirable'; but we are more likely to say 'Epicurus' ethical theory
is right', than 'Epicurus' ethical theory is true'; and it would seem
highly absurd to count truths and falsehoods in a book by Epicurus.)

The first of these conditions is much harder to fulfil than the
second. Most plain men do normally make ethical statements in a
fairly unsystematic way, without a very close and obvious relation
to an explicit underlying theory. On the other hand, as I shall argue,
ethical statements normally are closely related to performance; and
to abstract them from this involves wrenching them from their
normal context.

The relation which ethical statements normally do have with
performance can be seen most clearly if we examine the phenome-
non of ethical hypocrisy. Consider the example of a man who says
that murder is wrong, and at the same time secretly commits
murder with no qualms.

The comment that we normally make in such a case is that the
ethical pronouncements of the man conflict with his behaviour.
This is not to interpret the ethical pronouncements as describing
or predicting behaviour: the clearest indication of this is that we
are not inclined to label them false or incorrect in the light of the
man's behaviour. Instead, the conflict resembles that which we
perceive when a man promises to do something and then does the
opposite. The man has not lived up to what he said.

Ethical statements are related to performance in at least this
respect: they normally are interpreted as pledging that the person
who makes them will act, or try to act, accordingly. This is as true
of statements of value as it is of statements about what is right and
wrong. If someone says that aesthetic experiences are the most
valuable, and then spends all of his spare time in bowling and drink-
ing beer, resolutely avoiding concerts and poetry recitals, we say
that his behaviour conflicts with his words. The question of
hypocrisy arises, and we wonder whether he 'really meant' what he
said.

It is of course not the case that everyone whose actions and
behaviour do not entirely accord is a hypocrite. Broadly speaking,
we recognize that a man may sincerely make an ethical statement,
and yet at the moment of action yield to temptation. On the other
hand, there are some cases in which a man's actions and ethical
pronouncements do accord, and yet we judge the man to be a hypo-

crite. Someone who dwells on how good it is to give to charity, and who then gives to charity, may seem like a hypocrite if we suspect that his real motives are thoroughly selfish, as will the professed aesthete who appears to go to concerts for reasons of social prestige.

Clearly a crucial factor is our estimate of the strength of the inclination that accompanies the ethical judgment. If the accompanying inclination appears so very weak or negligible as to be easily overcome, or appears so weak that it does not provide anything like the dominant motive for acting in accordance with the ethical statement, then we judge that the agent is hypocritical. Gilbert Ryle puts a related point succinctly when he says of the difference between right and wrong, 'We are unwilling to allow that a person has learned this difference who does not, for instance, care a bit whether he breaks a promise or keeps it, and is quite indifferent as to whether anyone else is cruel or kind.'[1] A logical corollary of all of this is that behaviour which conflicts with one's ethical pronouncements calls for an explanation. There must have been (if one was sincere, and not hypocritical) factors strong enough to overcome a sincere desire to act in accordance with one's pronouncements. It is odd to say 'I did not act in the way I thought best' or 'I did not fulfil my obligation', *and* to deny that there is a reason for, or special cause of, this behaviour.

Kurt Baier recently has argued that the results of a man's evaluation of a solution to an ethical problem 'are logically separate from the "volition" which determines whether or not he will follow the guidance'.[2] There is this much truth to what Baier says: it is true that, say, a man may conclude, on the basis of ethical rules which he has been taught, that he ought not to commit murder, and yet may commit murder without any hesitation or qualms. It is true also that one cannot, without artificiality, draw a sharp line between concluding that one ought not to commit murder and believing that one ought not to commit murder. Yet in ordinary speech there is enough of a gradation so that it is clear that we normally would hesitate to say that the cheerful murderer really believes (or, except in a sociological or legal sense, knows) that murder is wrong, or to say (in Ryle's terms) that the man 'has learned' that he ought not to commit murder. If the man actually *says* that murder is wrong, this

---

[1] 'On Forgetting the Difference Between Right and Wrong', *Essays in Moral Philosophy*, ed. by A. I. Melden (Seattle: University of Washington Press, 1958), p. 155.
[2] 'Fact, Value and Norm in Stevenson's Ethics', *Nous*, Vol. 1 (1967), p. 156.

sharpens the conflict still further, thanks to the performatory quality of the utterance.

It is true that, to use an example of Baier's, Mrs Jones may correctly say, 'I know that we ought to save up money for Jack's education rather than spending the money on a vacation in the Bahamas', and at the same time favour spending the money on a vacation in the Bahamas. The point at which we begin to question whether Mrs Jones really believes (or knows) that she ought to save money for Jack's education, and at which we begin to question her sincerity, is the point at which it appears that she has no qualms or hesitation about spending the money designed for Jack's education on something else. We can reach that point easily enough, which suggests that what a man believes ethically, or can say sincerely, is *not* logically separable from the nature and strength of his volitions. If this removes an objection to Stevenson, we shall have (in the next chapter) to make our objections to Stevenson on other grounds.

None of the foregoing is to say that ethical statements are judged only in relation to behaviour. Indeed there are two standard ways of commenting adversely on a man's ethical statements. We can disagree with what he says, and assert that what he says is wrong or incorrect. Or we can comment on the relation between what he says and his attitudes, and accuse him of being insincere or hypocritical.

Because of this, accepting, or coming to believe, an ethical proposition cannot be viewed as a purely intellectual or theoretical activity. It involves a decision as to what will be viewed as correct, but it also involves a decision about that portion of one's life. Existentialist writers have surely been right in stressing the way in which ethical judgments function as commitments, and in pointing out how a choice of basic ethical beliefs is also to some extent a choice of the kind of person one will become.

Let us return to Moore. It is possible to consider ethical statements in abstraction from the attitudes and choices of the people who accept or reject them. It is possible to imagine, as it were, a detached ethical subject going through a check-list of ethical propositions, and checking them against his 'intuition'. This is only a slight caricature of the picture that Moore gives us, and of course it does enable him to speak without flagrant oddity of ethical propositions as true or false. It also leaves him with serious difficulties in determining the relation between ethical knowledge and conduct, or for that matter between propositions concerning goodness and propositions concerning what ought to be done.[1]

In sum, Moore's view that there is ethical truth, is tied to his tendency to treat ethical statements in abstraction from the dispositions and attitudes of the person who affirms them. This amounts to a one-sided view of ethics. It also leaves Moore open to the charge that, in order to portray ethics as cognitive, he ignored factors which would be damaging to his case. Part of my task will be to show that these factors can be accounted for within an argument that there is ethical knowledge.

[1] Cf. the essays by Paton and Frankena in *The Philosophy of G. E. Moore.*
The above criticism of Moore's view of ethical intuition of course does not apply to the 'intuitionism' of such philosophers as Sir W. David Ross, which has different strengths and weaknesses.

CHAPTER III
STEVENSON'S ETHICAL PHILOSOPHY

At the end of the last chapter I suggested that Moore was open to the accusation that, in order to portray ethics as 'cognitive', he ignored factors which would be damaging to his case. Someone who perceived the factors which Moore had ignored might well feel that their existence demonstrated that ethics was not entirely 'cognitive'. Something like this is implicit in Stevenson's remark that 'Moral judgments are concerned with *recommending* something for approval or disapproval; and this involves something more than a disinterested description. . . . In this way moral judgments go beyond cognition, speaking to the conative-affective natures of men.'[1]

We can take this as a starting point, for recognition both of Stevenson's contributions and his questionable assumptions. Of course one has to agree with Stevenson's statement, with some minor qualifications and one major qualification. Moral judgments often are concerned (among other things) with recommending something for approval or disapproval. They do involve something more than a disinterested description. They do speak to the conative-affective natures of men. Stevenson performed a valuable service in pointing these things out. But why does the fact that moral judgments fulfil all of these functions imply that they 'go beyond cognition'?

There is a familiar pair of assumptions at work here. They are as follows.

1. We can distinguish sharply between on one hand describing, explaining, predicting, etc. and on the other hand activities in the conative-affective realm, which include recommending, praising, insulting, condemning, etc.
2. Only activities of the first kind can be cognitive.

It should be pointed out, first of all, that there is no evidence that Moore did not share this pair of assumptions. That may well be one of the reasons why he gave such a one-sided picture of ethics. In order to maintain that ethics is cognitive he had to pre-

[1] *Ethics and Language* (New Haven: Yale University Press, 1960), p. 13; italics are Stevenson's.

sent ethical judgments as being purely descriptive: this especially enabled him to write his 'Prologomena to any future Ethics that can possibly pretend to be scientific'.

Let us examine the second of these assumptions. The first is somewhat vulnerable, since in everyday speech it is quite common to find 'conative-affective' elements in descriptive statements (e.g. 'The sky looks threatening', 'He is cruel'), and descriptive, predictive, or explanatory elements in evaluative statements (e.g. 'You are making a disastrous choice', 'He is cruel'). A good deal of this has been pointed out by Stevenson himself, who nevertheless did not let it impinge on the basic categories of his thinking. The second assumption however is extremely vulnerable. We can see this if we scan the ordinary uses of words with cognitive overtones, such as 'rational', 'reasonable' and 'intelligent'. These three words all have ordinary uses in cases pertaining primarily (if one maintains Stevenson's distinction) to the 'conative-affective' realm.

We speak of someone as being rational when he performs passably well at logical operations: when he can relate premises to a conclusion adequately well, and think through an argument of some complexity. But in many cases 'rational' also has connotations of 'not governed by emotions'. Thus we say that a king who has just been informed of the defection of a trusted general responds 'rationally' if he does not immediately fly into a rage, but instead lays plans to meet with the crisis. To respond rationally to a seductive offer involves weighing the consequences and one's obligations, instead of simply sinking into the mood of the moment.

If, however, we choose to give the word 'emotions' a sense as broad as the entire spectrum of the 'conative-affective', then of course we have to say that everyone always is governed by emotions. Given this sense of 'emotion', what we mean in the cases described by calling someone 'rational' is partly just that he is not governed by passionate emotions, but rather is governed by his calmer emotions. Part of the meaning also is that *what* emotions he feels, and also the relative strength of various emotions in his mood, will be determined partly by his experience and reflective judgment. (The further question of what 'conative-affective' element there is in what we normally call 'experience' and 'reflective judgment' is one which we will not here explore, although some things touching upon it will be said in Chapter VI.)

'Reasonable' and 'intelligent', like 'rational', have uses related to the realm of the 'conative-affective'. A reasonable man does not try to kill his enemies when he meets them on the street. He does not hope to become wealthy by betting at the racetrack. A man surely is being unreasonable if he asks new friends to sacrifice everything they possess for his sake. It is unreasonable also to neglect all of the sharp pleasures, excitement, and variety of life simply for the sake of a greater avoidance of pain. (Arguably, Epicurus was unreasonable.)

Someone whose wife has just deserted him can deal with the situation intelligently, if he makes suitable adjustments in his feelings and activities, or stupidly, if he fixes his hopes on impossible projects. Someone who has become wealthy can adjust to his new situation intelligently, if he spends his money wisely, or stupidly, if he spends his money foolishly. Someone who has taken a new job behaves intelligently if he responds cautiously to his co-workers, and behaves stupidly if he immediately loses his temper with all of his co-workers.

All of this serves to illustrate the point that actions, choices, and even emotional responses can be rational, reasonable, intelligent, or the opposites of these. Is there any reason to assume that ethical judgments, even if they involve important factors from the 'conative-affective' realm, cannot also be rational, reasonable, and intelligent?[1] Is there any reason to assume that, to the extent that they are 'conative-affective', they cannot be cognitive?

Stevenson's belief that moral judgments 'go beyond cognition' is related to his use of 'true' and 'false' in relation to ethics. Having criticized Moore's use, I shall now examine Stevenson's. If I can show oddities in Stevenson's use, this will help to establish a case that Stevenson, like Moore, gives a distorted picture of ethics. It also will help to build a case for saying that Stevenson's qualified and partial denial that ethics is 'cognitive' is not well-founded.

Stevenson's view of truth in ethics is quite complicated. In *Ethics and Language* he remarks that 'For the contexts that are most typical of normative ethics, the ethical terms have a function that is *both* emotive and descriptive.'[2] Application of ethical terms can give us information, e.g. it may be presumed that the 'good citizen' generally obeys laws. More fundamentally, an ethical statement tells us what the speaker approves of or disapproves of.

---

[1] Henry Aiken speaks ironically of Stevenson's 'tenacious desire to reserve the emotive meaning of such expressions as "rational" and "valid" for the processes of reasoning involved in formal logic and inductive science . . .'. *Reason and Conduct* (New York: Alfred A. Knopf, 1962), p. 62.

[2] *Ethics and Language*, p. 84; italics are Stevenson's.

Stevenson's view in *Ethics and Language* is that this 'descriptive meaning, which refers to the speaker's attitudes, may be true or false in the ordinary way'.[1] Stevenson also suggests in *Ethics and Language* that 'true' has a re-iterative function in ethics: to respond 'That is true' to another's ethical judgment is simply to concur.[2]

Stevenson's view appears to have shifted slightly by the dates of Essays 5 and 11 of *Facts and Values*. In Essay 5 he contrasts the 'so-called non-cognitive theory' of *Ethics and Language* with relativism. The ground of the contrast is that relativism interprets a man who makes an ethical judgment as expressing a belief about his attitude, whereas the Stevenson theory interprets him simply as expressing his attitude.[3] At the bottom of this contrast is a distinction, which is not apparent in *Ethics and Language*, between expressing an attitude and describing an attitude. If a man who makes an ethical judgment merely expresses his attitude, then it of course would be implausible to credit his statement with truth merely on the basis of its faithfully reporting his attitude. Accordingly, in Essay 11 of *Facts and Values* we find the two uses of 'true' in ethics which were provided for in *Ethics and Language* reduced to just one: the re-iterative one.[4]

The use, or uses, which Stevenson assigns to 'true' in ethical discourse are much less striking than the limitations which Stevenson places on these uses. My comments on Moore ought to have made it clear that I am not wedded to the word 'true': indeed I have argued that, when ethical statements are taken in context, 'right' or 'correct' usually would be a more appropriate word. However Stevenson's project is not to dispossess 'true' in favour of its relatives; and presumably the limitations he places on the use of 'true' would also be placed on the uses of 'right' or 'correct'. Thus my point will apply to all of these words: it will be that normally when they are used in ethical discourse, they are used without Stevenson's limitations.

Stevenson refuses to recognize what in Chapter II called an 'unqualified sense' of 'true' in ethics. In *Ethics and Language* the applicability of 'true' to an ethical judgment depends entirely either on the correspondence between the judgment and the attitudes of

[1] *ibid.*, p. 154.
[2] *ibid.*, p. 169.
[3] Cf. *Facts and Values* (New Haven: Yale University Press, 1963), pp. 80, 210. Cf. also 'Ethical Fallibility', in *Ethics and Society*, ed. by R. T. DeGeorge (New York: Anchor Books, 1966), p. 199.
[4] Cf. *Facts and Values*, pp. 214–20.

the person making the judgment, or on the agreement with the judgment which someone who is considering whether the judgment is 'true' feels. In *Facts and Values* again the applicability of 'true' to an ethical judgment is simply a matter of whether the person who is considering using 'true' agrees with the judgment or not.

Now clearly Stevenson has captured one dimension of our ordinary ethical use of 'true'. It is true that when Mr A. says 'Jones ought not to have done it', and Mr B replies 'That is true', the force of Mr B's reply is 'Jones ought not to have done it'.[1] 'That is true' does function as a repetition of what Mr A said. Indeed just how plausible Stevenson's account is in this respect can be seen when we appreciate the fact that, conversely, if Mr B. had replied, 'Indeed Jones ought not to have done it', this would have the force of Mr B's saying 'That is true'. More broadly, also, it is true that we normally call statements true if and only if we agree with them (unless, of course, we are concealing our opinion).

There simply is, however, more to the story than this. Most of us would argue that, when we say that 'Murder is generally wrong' is true, the truth of which we speak does not depend at all on our agreement with the claim. We are expressing our agreement, but we are not doing merely that. Stevenson speaks of the rule which determines the appropriateness of 'true' and 'false' in ethical discourse as 'purely syntactical'.[2] Most of us would consider that a purely syntactical account of our use of 'true' here leaves something out.

What of a world in which everyone approved of head-hunting? In such a world the judgment 'Head-hunting is generally wrong' would be considered false; it is equally clear that, in Stevenson's account, we could argue that the judgment still would be true, since the judgment 'It still would be true' after all simply reflects the agreement with the original judgment which we feel in contemplating the world in which it would be generally rejected. But does the matter simply end there? Is it, as it were, simply our opinion against theirs? Or are we entitled to say, not only that we are right and the head-hunters wrong (which Stevenson presumably would allow us to say, as expressing our agreement with ourselves), but also that head-hunting is wrong in a manner quite independent of what we happen to feel or agree with? Most of us would want to say this last. Most of us would deny that 'truth' here simply depends on

[1] *Facts and Values*, pp. 216–17.   [2] *ibid.*, p. 216.

what the person using the word agrees with. Most of us would deny that 'truth' here is assignable on the basis of a purely syntactical rule.

Because of the elements missing from Stevenson's picture of ethics, a careful commentator like Kerner can say of Stevenson, 'Moral judgments . . . were for him at bottom neither true nor false and incapable of logically contradicting one another.'[1] Furthermore Kerner can say that in Stevenson's theory 'the acceptability of a moral judgment became a purely arbitrary and subjective matter. He was unable to preserve the distinction between what merely seems good, or obligatory, and what really is so.'[2]

Throughout his career Stevenson very adroitly, although not entirely successfully, has attempted to protect himself against such accusations. As we have seen, he does assign 'true' at least one use in ethical discourse. He does recognise that there is ethical reasoning; although in *Ethics and Language*, he takes the view that 'The reasons which support or attack an ethical judgment . . . subject to some exceptions . . . are related to the judgment psychologically rather than logically'.[3] In *Ethical Fallibility*, his most disarming piece of writing, he even gives a plausible account in his terms of ethical doubt and indecision.[4]

Undoubtedly Stevenson always has been aware that his *kind* of position is paradoxical, and undoubtedly he has wished to minimize the paradox by subtle concessions to common sense on small points. In some ways he is reminiscent of the metaphysical idealist who eagerly says 'Of course material objects are *in a sense* real: I too believe in tables and chairs', and then expects common sense to be pacified. Specifically, for example, Stevenson, in distinguishing his position from that of Carnap and Ayer, suggests that we adopt a procedure which 'tempers the paradoxical contention that ethical

[1] *The Revolution in Ethical Theory* (Oxford: Oxford University Press, 1966), p. 99.

[2] *ibid.*, pp. 97–8.

[3] *Ethics and Language*, p. 113.

[4] The controversial edge of this essay is largely in the familiar claim that, whereas scientific claims express beliefs, ethical judgments express attitudes (and not beliefs). By now, however, 'belief' has achieved the status of a technical term in Stevenson's philosophy, so that it is hard to be entirely sure what it is that Stevenson is claiming. My own view is that ethical statements normally express attitudes *and* express beliefs about what is good, bad, right, or wrong, etc. The two are closely related. To disapprove of something is to believe that it is bad.

judgments are 'neither true nor false'.[1] It is partly because of this that we are granted the re-iterative use of 'true' in ethics.

To the extent that philosophy consists of 'assembling reminders for a particular purpose', we ought to remind ourselves about certain features of our ordinary use of 'true', 'right' and 'correct' in ethical discourse. One is that we do, after all, normally interpret these uses to be what I have called 'unqualified'. As Carl Wellman says, not only do we judge some ethical judgments to be correct, but also 'the notion of correctness brings with it the assumption that correctness or incorrectness of a proposed answer is fixed independently of anyone's acceptance or rejection. In some sense the answer is there to be discovered; thinking cannot make it so.'[2] It is worth reminding ourselves of the ways in which, as Peter Glassen has elegantly argued, ordinary ethical discourse is 'redolent of cognitivity'.[3]

There is a fine point to be considered here. It could be argued that in fact ordinary language is neither 'cognitivist' nor 'non-cognitivist', neither 'Stevensonian' nor 'anti-Stevensonian', and that it is common sense rather than ordinary language itself which provides the ammunition upon which both Wellman and Glassen rely. Ordinary language, the argument might run, does normally express ethical judgments in declarative form, and does allow us to speak of them as 'correct' or 'incorrect': but after all Stevenson has acknowledged these facts and has interpreted them in his way. Stevenson's difficulty, if it is one, is not that there is anything in ordinary language which shows him to be wrong. It is rather that the interpretation which he gives of what is found in ordinary language runs counter to the 'common sense' interpretation which most people are inclined to give. But after all, the argument might conclude, that just shows how people have been confused by the old philosophies.

My own view is this: one can distinguish between what I previously called the 'surface facts' of ordinary language (that people do speak of ethical judgments as 'correct' etc.) and that portion of ordinary language which is exposed when people are asked those questions which in philosophy constitute test cases. For example, if someone in a reflective mood says 'I am trying to find the correct

---

[1] *Ethics and Language*, p. 267.

[2] 'Emotivism and Ethical Objectivity', *American Philosophical Quarterly*, Vol. 5 (1968), p. 98.

[3] 'The Cognitivity of Moral Judgments', *Mind*, Vol. LXVIII (1959), p. 71.

answer to this ethical problem: I know that there is an answer which is correct and will be correct regardless of whether I come to accept it or not, and that is why I am thinking so hard about the problem', this is a piece of ordinary language, albeit a sophisticated piece. After all, 'ordinary language' does not mean 'frequently used language': 'ordinary' merely is opposed to 'technical', 'conditioned by special definitions', or to 'language which in normal contexts would be odd or inappropriate'. Thus there appears to be no ground for a very sharp distinction between ordinary language and common sense interpretations of ordinary language. If we retain the broad sense of 'ordinary language', it is clear that as things now stand ordinary ethical discourse does go against Stevenson, in the manner in which Glassen and Wellman have indicated.

It is clear also that Stevenson has known this for some time. He apparently has felt, however, that this character of his work was justified by the somewhat confused character of ordinary ethical discourse. In some places Stevenson seems to say that ordinary ethical discourse is somewhat confused in the sense of presenting a picture which is not very neat: less neat than one would want a finished philosophical theory to be. Thus in *Ethics and Language* he says that his working models 'will not be adequate to the subtleties of common usage, . . . but they will preserve in rough form much that is essential to ethical analysis . . .'.[1] In *The Philosophy of G. E. Moore*, on the other hand, he had suggested that ordinary ethical discourse does not embody a decision on a crucial point: 'In my opinion, the ethical terms are in fact used so vaguely that people *have not decided* whether 'X is right' said by A, and 'X is not right' said by B, are to be taken as incompatible or not . . .'.[2] Elsewhere in *Ethics and Language* Stevenson suggests that ethical discourse sometimes embodies an incorrect philosophical theory, one such as Moore's: 'The ethical terms are sometimes used hypostatically. . . . If this hypostatization is persistent, and increases the emotional effect of "good", it may occasion (for the usage of certain people) an emotive meaning that is dependent on confused meaning.'[3] Professor C. Schuster says that Stevenson wrote to her in 1952 saying, 'my two patterns of analysis in *Ethics and Language* do not give an account of what ordinary people

[1] *Ethics and Language*, p. 21.
[2] *The Philosophy of G. E. Moore*, ed. P. Schilpp (New York: Tudor, 1952), p. 84; italics are Stevenson's.
[3] *Ethics and Language*, p. 88.

normally mean when they use the ethical terms'.[1] However common usage, according to Stevenson, is 'confused': his work was intended to 'salvage' from what people meant 'all that I, viewing the situation from an empirical viewpoint, could find intelligible . . .'.[2]

The last quotation is especially revealing. Stevenson was not drawn to his theory simply by the character of ordinary ethical discourse: it suggests that there may have been overriding reasons, quite separate from the character of ordinary ethical discourse, which led Stevenson to accept his theory. These reasons clearly are related to the modern forms of empiricism. Professor Schuster herself endorses the 'non-cognitive theory of ethics' as a 'corollary' of an epistemology which she associates with logical positivism.[3] It seems to me that there is adequate warrant for considering the background of Stevenson's ethical philosophy to be very much like this.

Of course Stevenson's view can be defended on yet other grounds. It might be argued that while Stevenson's theory is not faithful to ordinary language, it is a 'prescriptive' linguistic proposal which, since it denies suprapersonal authority to our ethical judgments, has the virtue of encouraging us to be more tolerant. Or a theory of the general character of Stevenson's can be defended, as it has been by Frederick Olafson, in terms of its effect on our moral life, in making us view moral judgment as more a kind of doing than of witnessing or reporting.[4]

Olafson is clearly right in suggesting that acceptance of a theory of the general character of Stevenson's might well have an effect on the way we hold our moral views. Whether these effects would be good or bad however is open to question. They might, I suspect, be admirable (in the manner Olafson describes) in the case of people who took ethical questions seriously to begin with (including presumably professional philosophers), and rather unfortunate in the case of people who to begin with were not inclined to think much

---

[1] *Mind*, Vol. LXX (1961), p. 95, italics in the text.

[2] *ibid.*, pp. 95–6.

[3] *ibid.*, p. 95.

[4] 'Meta-Ethics and the Moral Life', *Philosophical Review*, Vol. LXV (1956). Olafson admits that 'the emotive theory is not a correct explication of the way certain terms occuring in moral arguments are actually used and understood' (p. 171). At the end of his generally very subtle and penetrating essay, he suggests that the emotive theory might be presented 'as an account of what we are *really* doing' in making moral judgments. I cannot understand whether this means that there is empirical evidence which counts for the emotive theory and against its rivals, or instead is another way of putting the prescriptive protest against our ordinary way of describing moral judgment.

about questions of value. These latter might feel that, if there are no independently correct answers to ethical problems, they could not in a sense go wrong: this might increase their tendency not to concern themselves with ethical problems, which in turn might have an adverse effect on the degree of focus of their lives.[1] Some of my remarks in Chapter V about the good and bad effects of large numbers of people accepting relativism would apply, I think, to the effects of large numbers of people accepting a meta-ethic like Stevenson's.

In any event Stevenson has never, to my knowledge, suggested that we adopt his ethical philosophy because of the good practical effects of adopting it. Instead his argument has always rested on purely philosophical grounds, to the effect that his account has the weight of philosophical considerations behind it. Whether this is so depends on whether it is reasonable for us to reject, on empiricist grounds, the 'cognitivist' assumptions embedded in ordinary language. This we must now consider.

---

[1] It is arguable also that people who accept an 'objective' ethic may be conscious of their own fallibility in a laudable way. Cf. H. D. Lewis, 'Obedience to Conscience', *Mind*, Vol. LIV (1945).

CHAPTER IV

A. J. AYER

We may ask 'On what philosophical grounds would a philosopher feel compelled to adopt an analysis of ethical language which in effect denied the existence of ethical knowledge?' A. J. Ayer is the philosopher who most clearly and forcefully stated these grounds, and we can get close to the roots of our problem by examining Ayer's ethical philosophy. In moving from Stevenson to Ayer, I am not suggesting that Stevenson accepted everything that Ayer said, or even that Stevenson shared all of Ayer's basic assumptions. But certainly Stevenson accepted the *kind* of approach to ethics which Ayer stood for, and an examination of Ayer's assumptions and arguments is highly relevant to Stevenson's position. Indeed it is highly relevant to the position of almost every philosopher who in the last thirty years has opposed 'cognitivist' views in ethics.

The account of ethics which Ayer gives in *Language Truth and Logic* is based ultimately on one principle, the logical positivist principle of verification. One of Ayer's formulations of the principle goes as follows: 'A statement is held to be literally meaningful if and only if it is either analytic or empirically verifiable.'[1] Statements which are verifiable, Ayer says, may be divided into those which are directly verifiable and those which are indirectly verifiable. 'A statement is directly verifiable if it is either itself an observation statement, or is such that in conjunction with one or more observation statements it entails at least one observation statement which is not deducible from these other premises alone . . .'. A statement is 'indirectly verifiable if it satisfies the following conditions: first, that in conjunction with certain other premises it entails one or more directly verifiable statements which are not deducible from these other premises alone; and secondly, that these other premises do not include any statement that is not either analytic, or directly verifiable, or capable of being independently established as indirectly verifiable.'[2]

If we apply this principle to ethics, we get the following result. Ethical statements have to be analytic, or empirically verifiable, or

[1] *Language Truth and Logic*, second edition (New York: Dover Books, 1947), p. 9.
[2] *ibid.*, p.13.

they are literally meaningless. Now Ayer recognizes that typically there are both analytic statements and empirically verifiable statements within books of ethics. Ethics books often include 'propositions which express definitions of ethical terms, or judgments about the legitimacy or possibility of certain definitions', and also 'propositions describing the phenomena of moral experience, and their causes'.[1] The former propositions are logical; the latter 'must be assigned to the science of psychology, or sociology'.[2] Ayer is concerned primarily not with these propositions, but with 'actual ethical judgments'.[3] In relation to these, Ayer argues that one cannot reduce 'the whole sphere of ethical terms' to non-ethical terms, and thus that 'in our language, sentences which contain normative ethical symbols are not equivalent to sentences which contain psychological propositions, or indeed empirical propositions of any kind'.[4] Thus 'actual ethical judgments' are not equivalent to empirically verifiable propositions. Ayer does not examine seriously the possibility that ethical judgments might be analytic; but the aforementioned argument, of course, could be used to show that fundamental ethical judgments (e.g. 'Pleasure is good') cannot be regarded as true by definition, and hence are not analytic. If ethical judgments are not analytic, and are not empirically verifiable, then they are not literally meaningful. Hence they fall in a category with poetry and metaphysics. It follows from this that ethics, at least those parts of ethics which cannot be assigned to logic, psychology, or sociology, cannot contain truth or embody knowledge. Ayer's conclusion indeed is that 'ethical judgments are mere expressions of feeling, there can be no way of determining the validity of any ethical system, and indeed, no way of asking whether any such system is true'.[5] Ethical judgments, according to Ayer, 'have no validity'.[6]

I

A first comment on Ayer's formulation and use of the verification principle might run as follows. Ayer applies a standard to other putative branches of non-logical knowledge which was designed to fit the sciences. In this sense Ayer is a philosophical Procrustes, forcing ethics, theology, metaphysics, etc., to lie in an inflexible conceptual bed.

[1] *ibid.*, p. 103.   [2] *loc. cit.*   [3] *loc. cit.*   [4] *ibid.*, pp. 104, 105.
[5] *ibid.*, p. 112.   [6] *ibid.*, p. 110.

It is impossible to discuss this without noting the enormous prestige of the sciences in this century. It is true that, in this century, when most people think of non-logical knowledge they think of scientific knowledge. Not only have scientists very often solved the problems which they consider most worth solving; but also the technical achievements which have followed from some of these solutions have made everyone aware, in very concrete ways, of the success of science.

Scientific knowledge is widely thought of as having two salient features. One is that scientific disputes are all capable, at least in theory, of being resolved experimentally. That is, at least in theory, scientists can design, or at least expect to be able to design, experiments, such that all competent observers who witness the results of the experiments will in the long run adopt the same side of the argument. Thus scientific theories, however abstract sounding, are capable of being verified or falsified concretely.

The account of science in the last paragraph is no doubt over-simple. In cases in which two theories can accommodate the same data, or in which a scientific issue is mainly one relating to theory construction, it would be over-simple to say that the issues can be resolved on a purely experimental basis. But the previous paragraph at least represents the image that most educated people have of science. It is arguably not a thorough distortion of science, but more important is that it is the most widely entertained image.

The second salient feature which scientific knowledge is widely considered to have is closely connected to the first. Because scientific problems can be settled concretely, they do get settled. In the short run, there may be sharp division of expert opinion as to whether, say, Einstein's theory is correct or not; but in the long run the experts will agree.[1] This situation is often contrasted to the one in philosophy, where experts still bicker about problems on which Plato and Aristotle worked. It is also contrasted to the one in ethics, in which intelligent, thoughtful people maintain widely divergent opinions as to which way of life is best, or as to the rightness or wrongness of certain kinds of actions.

---

[1] The long run of course may be rather long. It is worth recalling Max Planck's famous remark that 'a new scientific truth does not triumph by convincing its opponents and making them see the light, but rather because its opponents eventually die, and a new generation grows up that is familiar with it'. *Scientific Autobiography*, pp. 33–4, quoted in Thomas S. Kuhn, *The Structure of Scientific Revolutions* (Chicago: The University of Chicago Press Phoenix Edition, 1966), p. 150.

The differing degrees of consensus in science and in ethics have tremendous significance in view of the intellectual laziness which causes men to search for a 'deep underlying structure', and thus to over-simplify. It is tempting to believe that there must be only one kind of knowledge, apart from that provided by logical analysis. It is very natural, considering the enormous prestige which science currently has, to take scientific knowledge as the model for all non-logical knowledge. Ayer works this out in an especially transparent way. This can be seen by examining what he means by 'verification'.

The word 'verification' is sometimes used in a broad sense such that to verify a statement is to ascertain its truth or correctness. In this broad sense, metaphysicians often claim to verify their theories by tricky-sounding arguments, or by a 'light of nature', or some such device. Also in this broad sense, Moore in effect maintained that we can verify an ethical judgment by means of our 'intuition'. According to Moore, if we wish to know for example whether appreciation of beauty is valuable, we must rely on intuition.

Plainly these kinds of 'verification' will not satisfy Ayer. There are two reasons. One is that they are not 'empirical verification'. Moore's intuitions, for example, are not expressed in 'observation statements', nor do they have the logical relations to observation statements which Ayer requires. We might remark here that Ayer nowhere argues that verification of non-logical claims which lacks this relation to observation statement is illegitimate: he simply assumes this.

The second reason is that verification, in Ayer's terms, is not grounded merely on the views of one individual. There is an implicit appeal to consensus. Thus he says of a theory like Moore's,

'A feature of this theory, which is seldom recognized by its advocates, is that it makes statements of value unverifiable. For it is notorious that what seems intuitively certain to one person may seem doubtful or even false, to another. So that unless it is possible to provide some criterion by which one may decide between con-flicting intuitions, a mere appeal to intuition is worthless as a test of a proposition's validity. But in the case of moral judgments no such criterion can be given.'[1]

Now of course Moore would assert that there is a 'criterion by which one may decide between conflicting intuitions', namely one's

---

[1] *Language Truth and Logic, op. cit., p.* 106.

own intuition. If this will not satisfy Ayer, it is because Ayer wishes a criterion which can be used to more general satisfaction.

Thus what Ayer means by 'verification', in relation to non-logical claims, is a process which, by no coincidence, involves the two salient features which scientific knowledge is generally considered to have. That is, verification (of non-logical claims) has to be in terms of concrete processes (i.e. the verifiable statements have either to be observation statements or to have the proper logical relations with observation statements). Also verification has to be able to lead to general agreement among competent observers. If there is no test which is able to resolve conflicts, there is no genuine verification.

Here we have swung around in a circle. There is scientific knowledge, but not ethical knowledge, because the claims of science are capable of empirical verification, but ethical claims are not capable of empirical verification. What is empirical verification? It is the way questions are settled in science.

In other words, ethics is not science. It should not be surprising that ethical knowledge cannot meet Ayer's test: the test was designed with scientific knowledge specifically in mind, and was designed narrowly. It must be admitted that ethical knowledge is significantly different from scientific knowledge. But to say this does not imply that ethical knowledge cannot qualify as 'knowledge'.

II

This will do as a first comment only. It is true that Ayer's central argument rests on important unargued assumptions, but it is true that he raises disturbing points. It is disturbing that ethical disagreements seem incapable of being settled concretely, and that they so often seem incapable of being settled at all.

Let us examine the first point briefly, and the second point at some length. With regard to the relation between ethics and 'observation', it first should be said that it is pointless, and exasperatingly mysterious, to try to get around the difficulty by speaking of a 'moral sense' which provides solutions to moral problems. As Schlick remarked, 'The moral sense is merely assumed; its organs cannot be pointed out as can the human eye.'[1]

Ayer also seems clearly right when he argues that in our language

[1] What Is The Aim of Ethics', trans. by David Rynin, *Logical Positivism*, ed. A. J. Ayer (New York: The Free Press, 1959), p. 252.

normative sentences in general cannot be translated into sentences which merely make psychological claims, or claims which would be contained in other sciences. (One qualification which I would like to impose on this has been suggested in Chapter I: some normative sentences might have a place in a 'value-ridden' psychology.) I already have expressed my (highly qualified) agreement with Moore concerning the naturalistic fallacy: so that I shall not seek 'a way out' by arguing that what appear to be ethical claims are really just scientific claims. Indeed, such an argument would be suicidal for ethics, since it would imply that what might appear to be ethical knowledge is actually scientific knowledge.

In Chapter VI, I shall adopt instead a third approach, which I merely indicate now. I shall argue that experience, including what perforce must be called sensory experience, does enter into ethical judgment, and does in many cases provide supporting evidence for ethical statements. The character of this experience in many cases demands special interpretation, and the logical relations between ethical statements and the experiences which support them are in general not simple. But my argument does add up to the claim that many ethical statements are 'verified' concretely by means of observation.

The rub is that many of the cases in which I can show that experience plays a major role in ethical judgment are cases in which experiences are unlikely to be shared by people of a wide variety of outlooks. To give now just one example: we may, as a result of seeing the lives of poor negro children in the South, conclude that government food surpluses ought to be distributed more widely. But an extremely zealous white segregationist may, in viewing the same events, 'see' something different, and incidentally arrive at a different ethical judgment. In contrast to the experience which is most closely related to ethical judgment, the experience which is most commonly required in the laboratory seems 'stripped down' and geared to the lowest common denominator of our perceptual ability. (There are exceptions to this: some perceptions which occur in the laboratory require tremendous skill, skill which is generally recognized. But to perceive the emptiness of someone's life is very different from reading a dial.)

If ethical experience often is not shared, then my argument in Chapter VI, while it may do a great deal to deal with the first point, will not do as much to deal with the second. Why is it that ethical disputes so often seem incapable of being settled? Does this disability of ethical statements disqualify them from embodying knowledge?

A number of writers have argued that ethical disagreement of a fundamental kind is less common than often is thought. Solomon Asch, for example, arguing against the claims of cultural relativists, says that 'It seems rather that certain ethical discriminations are universally known. We still have to hear of a society to which modesty, courage, and hospitality are not known.'[1] However, it remains the case that there *are* fundamental ethical disagreements, even among highly respectable people, which are not readily able to be settled to general satisfaction. D. H. Munro has pointed out that the value judgments of St Augustine and G. E. Moore are in many respects quite opposite.[2] Anyone surveying our contemporary scene must be impressed by the depth and frequency of ethical differences, even just within America.

We may observe that ethics has looked somewhat different at different times. Any reader of Hume's ethical works cannot help but be struck by the fact that Hume assumes the general agreement of mankind on basic ethical points. 'All mankind', he says, 'so far resemble the good principle, that where interest or revenge or envy perverts not our disposition, we are always inclined, from our natural philanthropy, to give the preference to the happiness of society, and consequently to virtue above its opposite.'[3] This is not simply the result of Hume's well-known cheerfulness. One gets the impression that almost all of the people Hume knew *did* agree on basic ethical points. Ethical diversity was not as prominent in eighteenth-century England as it is in the twentieth-century world. With regard to basic ethical points, almost everyone 'saw things the same way'.

Hume of course knew both of primitive tribes (such as the ancient Scythians) and of civilized satanists (or people like Nero, if his cruelty 'be allowed entirely voluntary').[4] But the ethical findings of these people did not loom large in his thinking. The major reason was that their findings could be dismissed: the people were in a sense not fully human. The passion for martial bravery among the

[1] 'A Critique of the Psychology of Cultural Relativism', *Values and Obligation*, ed. Richard B. Brandt (New York: Harcourt, Brace & World, 1961), p. 483.

[2] Cf. *Empiricism and Ethics* (Cambridge: Cambridge University Press, 1967), p. 22.

[3] *An Enquiry Concerning the Principles of Morals* (La Salle, Illinois: The Open Court Publishing Co., 1953), p. 62.

[4] *An Enquiry Concerning the Principles of Morals*, p. 62.

Scythians had 'destroyed the sentiments of humanity'; 'absolute, unprovoked, disinterested malice' in a man would 'pervert . . . the feelings of humanity'.[1] Hume speaks of the 'uncultivated nations, who have not as yet had full experience of the advantages attending beneficence, justice, and the social virtues . . .'.[2] Hume's attitude towards Nero and the Scythians was very much the attitude that a scientist would take towards people who are so cross-eyed or feeble minded that they cannot properly read the gauges in the laboratory.

This assured response to the ethical views of primitive peoples and civilized malcontents can be found even into the twentieth century. As late as 1912, Prichard felt that he could meet the objection that 'obligations cannot be self-evident, since many actions regarded as obligations by some are not so regarded by others' by remarking that 'the appreciation of an obligation is, of course, only possible for a developed moral being, and that different degrees of development are possible'.[3]

This suggests that there are factors in the social climate of the mid-twentieth century which make Ayer's points seem more disturbing than they might have at other times. I wish to make two points about the difference in degree of irreducible disagreement between ethics and science. One is that this difference is contingent, and not strictly implied by the nature of ethics.[4] The other is that there is no corresponding difference in the possibilities of strict logical proof in the two subjects: scientific claims are, in formal deductive terms, just as unprovable as ethical claims. When these two points have been made, we shall have Ayer's points regarding verification in better perspective.

The first point may be approached by means of an extreme and odd case. Mr X claims that he sees an elephant across the room from him. None of us sees the elephant. We disagree with Mr X as to its presence. Let us suppose also that the disagreement cannot be explained in any of the most obvious ways. Mr X is not drunk;

---

[1] *ibid.*, pp. 91, 62.   [2] *ibid.*, pp. 91–2.

[3] 'Does Moral Philosophy Rest on a Mistake?' *Mind*, N.S. Vol. XXI (1912), pp. 29–30.

[4] Alan Gewirth has indicated a harder line than mine is here. Cf. 'Positive "Ethics" and Normative "Science"', *Philosophical Review*, Vol. 69 (1960). I do agree with many of his points, and especially that the contrast between ethics and science has been overdrawn. But it seems to me that even if we were to give parallel definitions of what we were to count as 'ethics' and as 'science'—in terms let us say of what was endorsed by holders of Ph.D. degrees—we would find a good deal more diversity in ethics than in science.

he is not drugged; he is not under hypnosis. He may, however, be mentally deranged; although the chief sympton of derangement (if that is what he has) is his insistence that he sees an elephant.

There are various ways in which we might try to convince Mr X that he is wrong. We might call in other people, all of whom insist they do not see the elephant. Sometimes this is very persuasive, and the dissenter sheepishly admits that he 'must be seeing things'. But let us suppose also that it does not work in this case. Let us suppose also that when we all go forward to touch the supposed elephant, Mr X claims to feel the elephant whereas the rest of us feel nothing.

At this stage we might take a photograph of the area in which the elephant supposedly is, and show it to Mr X. This very often is persuasive. X may look at the photograph, acknowledge that it is blank, and admit that he must have made a mistake. But let us suppose instead that he looks at the photograph, and claims to see an elephant on what the rest of us regard as blank.

Imagine also that we bring along a device which measures the weight of objects in that part of the room in which X claims to see the elephant. The pointer stays at zero, indicating that there is nothing heavier than air there. This may convince X. He may look at the dial, and admit his mistake. But let us suppose that he looks at the dial, and claims that the pointer is at a very high number instead of at zero. Throughout all of the tests that we perform *vis-à-vis* the elephant, he perceives the results of the tests differently from us, and claims with apparent sincerity that they support his view.

This example may seem far-fetched, and indeed it is: such things rarely happen. It would be rash however to suggest that they never happen. Take for example a case which may bear some analogy to the case of Mr X: the apparitions at Lourdes. It is possible that the evidence which convinces the pious that the apparitions occurred will never convince the sceptic, and that what the sceptic considers to be evidence will never convince the pious. It is conceivable, for example, that if the sceptic were to have a photograph of the scene which he claimed revealed no apparition, a pious person either might feel able to distinguish the suggestive outline of an apparition in the murky background of the photograph, or might point out that apparitions do not project themselves into photographs.

There are no logical considerations which show that a case like that of Mr X could not happen. Indeed there is no logical contradiction in the idea of a world in which there are a number of people like Mr X, each with a different sort of peculiar perception. Thus the fact that our world is on the whole not like this, that there is on the whole general agreement on scientific data, is contingent. Moreover—and this is the main point—it is contingent that our methods of scientific verification by and large work, that we can distinguish a class of competent judges and can expect agreement among them.

Conversely, it is a contingent fact that there is as much ethical disagreement as there is, and that our methods for settling ethical disagreements often do not work. One could imagine a world which consisted of just one society, in which there were far tighter social bonds of ethical consensus than existed even in Hume's England. In such a world there would be recognized methods, available to everyone, for settling ethical problems to the satisfaction of everyone; and it would be very hard indeed to withhold the word 'verification' from these methods. There is no logical contradiction in such an idea.

My second point also may be illustrated by the case of Mr X. There is no deductive logical proof which strictly can prove that Mr X is wrong. If there were such a proof, its premises would have to be based on experience; and we cannot prove that Mr X ought to have the same experience that we have. Indeed it is always barely conceivable that Mr X is right. There is the infinitesimal chance that everyone but him has been hypnotized in some undetected way, or has been deceived by a Cartesian evil demon. We could, conceivably, emerge from our spell and find that Mr X is right.

Logically Mr X is on a par with a sadist who consistently argues that torturing innocent people is good. Extremely plausible arguments may be offered against both of them. The experience and judgment of mankind oppose them, but there is no strict deductive proof that they are wrong.

Of course we often use the word 'proof' in a much looser sense than the one which implies strict deductive proof. We speak loosely of proving that iron is heavier than water, that elephants are not native to Connecticut, and that crime does not pay.

In this loose sense, proofs are common in science and uncommon in ethics. But what does this sense involve? it involves, roughly, using recognized procedures to arrive at answers upon which all competent judges will agree.

In a society in which ethical judgments and ethically relevant experiences are as various as in ours, there are not always very generally 'recognized procedures' for arriving at ethical answers. It is sometimes hard to define who ethically 'competent judges' would be, and on many ethical questions it would be foolish to expect agreement among a cross-section of educated people. So that the fact that what is loosely called 'proof' is common in science and uncommon in ethics reduces to the familiar fact that there appears to be more irreducible disagreement within ethics than there is in science. This, I have argued, is contingent.

III

It is worth reminding ourselves that Ayer clearly is wrong when he says that in ethics it is not possible 'to provide some criterion by which one may decide between conflicting intuitions.' There are criteria. If X claims to intuit that progressive taxation is good, and Y claims to intuit that it is undesirable, Z may apply the criterion of the general welfare (or 'the greatest happiness of the greatest number') and thus decide in X's favour. If X claims to intuit that Mr A, who is charming but extremely cruel and irresponsible, leads a good life, and Y claims to intuit the opposite, Z may apply the criterion of contribution to human welfare (or of decency to other people) and thus decide in Y's favour.

Of course it must be added that there are conflicting criteria that may be applied to a case. We may apply the criterion of lack of dullness to Mr A's life, and decide thus that it is good. An argument between W and Z as to the goodness of Mr A's life probably would never be settled.

The fact that our criteria may not be universally accepted, however, does not prevent most of us from using them. It is important to realize that there are ways of deciding difficult ethical questions: most of us do not simply pick an answer out of the blue, or guess. One major difference between the use of criteria in ethics and their use in science comes around again to the difference in disagreement within the two subjects. Whether this should affect their 'cognitivity' is a matter which we can explore by raising two questions.

The first question is this. Imagine a world in which people like Mr X (who persists in seeing the elephant) are extremely common, and people like today's scientific observers are extremely uncommon. Let us suppose indeed that in this world the sub-community of people who by our present standards are competent scientific observers is very small, and that it is regarded by all of the others as eccentric. Given the limited group for whom scientific questions could be 'settled', would Ayer wish to say that in such a world there would be scientific 'verification' and scientific knowledge?

One cannot be certain what Ayer would answer to such a question, but I suspect that his answer would be 'Yes'. He could point out that the scientifically competent observers would (under the terms of the hypothesis) still be able to identify one another, maintain standards, and thus carry out 'objective' tests of scientific claims. Indeed it would sound odd to say that scientific knowledge would disappear merely as a result of competent observers' being outnumbered by a variety of eccentrics and lunatics.

The second question is this. Imagine a world in which there are small groups of people who share ethical assumptions and general ethical outlooks. Within these groups certain criteria for settling ethical questions are universally accepted, and within the groups there also tends to be widespread agreement on the manner of applying these criteria. Thus these groups, in relation to the larger society, have the same cohesiveness and single-mindedness with regard to settling ethical questions that the small minority of scientific observers had in the world of our first question. Do we then say that for these groups there would be ethical 'verification' and ethical knowledge?

The question may be put into perspective if we realize that the world imagined is very much like our world. Convinced utilitarian hedonists and zealous, obedient Roman Catholics form two such groups in our world. Within these groups there is basic agreement as to how to settle ethical questions. If one accepts the ethical assumptions of one of these groups, then one believes that there are 'objective' tests of ethical claims.

From the viewpoint of a thoroughly convinced utilitarian hedonist, then, the position of utilitarian hedonists in our world must seem very similar to the position of the small minority of scientifically competent observers in the first world. It would seem to him absurd to credit the scientifically competent observers in the first world with 'verification' of their claims and with knowledge, and yet to deny that there is ethical verification and ethical knowledge in our world.

At this point we are getting down to the level of very basic assumptions, first responses, and philosophical prejudices. On this level many people might respond by saying, 'But the small minority of scientifically competent observers would be clearly right; it is not entirely clear which ethical group in our society is right.' However, in terms of our example, it is not at all clear to Mr X that the 'scientifically competent' observers are right. Furthermore if we put the difference between the scientists and the ethical groups in terms of differing degrees to which we may be confident of correctness, then we are saying that ethical statements may be correct in somewhat the sense in which scientific claims may be correct, only that we are more confident in the case of the scientific claims. For an ethical 'cognitivist', as I pointed out in Chapter I, this is more than half of the battle: once it is admitted that ethical statements may be unqualifiedly correct, he can go on (if he wishes) to argue that in some cases apprehension of a correct ethical statement qualifies as knowledge.

Ayer I think would respond by saying that, in the case of the convinced utilitarian hedonist, 'what seems to be an ethical judgment is . . . a factual classification of an action as belonging to some class of actions by which a certain moral attitude on the part of the speaker is habitually aroused'.[1] Ayer does say that 'a man who is a convinced utilitarian may simply mean by calling an action right that it tends to promote, or more probably that it is the sort of action that tends to promote, the general happiness; and in that case the validity of his statement becomes an empirical matter of fact'.[2] But this is too easy a way of avoiding difficulties. Ayer suggests (on the same page) that he would say the same kind of thing about, say, the zealous and obedient Roman Catholic that he does about the utilitarian. Thus, if Ayer followed this line of thought, he would have to say that when the Roman Catholic claims that birth control is wrong he is merely making a factual claim that birth control is included among the actions prohibited by the Church. The utilitarian who endorses birth control would presumably merely be making the factual claim that birth control falls within the class of actions which tend to promote the general happiness. If this is so, and if the Roman Catholic is also willing to concede that in fact happiness would be promoted by the immoral activity of birth control, then the utilitarian and the Roman Catholic do not really disagree. One condemns, and the other praises, birth control; but the only claims that they are making are factual claims, which do not contradict one another. This plainly would be an absurd con-

[1] *Language Truth and Logic, op. cit.*, p. 21.   [2] *loc. cit.*

clusion. In ordinary language the Roman Catholic and the utilitarian would be said to be contradicting one another. Furthermore, both zealous Roman Catholics and utilitarians themselves would say that their claim about birth control was more than just a factual claim: they are claiming that *because* birth control fits a certain classification it is right, or wrong as the case may be.

If the utilitarian and the Roman Catholic are making normative rather than merely factual claims, then are we to deny that their claims are literally meaningful? Ayer says that we are. We have examined the roots of Ayer's assumptions, and have seen that his denial of literal meaning to ethics stems from two points: that ethical disagreements seem incapable of being settled concretely (as scientific disagreements can be), and that ethical disagreements often seem incapable of being settled at all. With some qualifications I have conceded the second of these points (although I have argued that the difference in degree of long-range consensus between ethics and science is merely a contingent, rather than a logical matter). To concede this point, however, is not to agree that Ayer is justified in making as much of it as he does.

At the root of Ayer's denial of literal meaning to ethics is his view that ethics is too different from science and logic to constitute knowledge. Very broadly, a large part of the argument in the last three chapters of this book will be that there are important similarities between ethics and subjects which even Ayer would consider branches of knowledge, and that these similarities are important enough to justify speaking of ethical knowledge. This would lead to the complaint against Ayer that he made too much of the differences, and not enough of the similarities.

CHAPTER V

RELATIVISM

In the last two chapters we have examined positions which have argued in effect, purely on logical and philosophical grounds, that there is no ethical knowledge. In the three chapters following this one I shall argue, mainly on philosophical grounds, that there is ethical knowledge. Before I do this, however, I must complete examination of the negative case. The case against saying that there is ethical knowledge does not exist merely on the highest philosophical level: it exists also in a climate of ethical opinion, in the Western world (especially in America) in the twentieth century, which is increasingly sceptical about ethics. In other words, the negative case does not consist merely of logical and philosophical arguments: it also may rely on an ethical orientation which finds 'absolutist' ethics repressive. This remaining element of the case against ethical knowledge can best be examined by examining relativism.

A discussion of relativism both has, and lacks, relevance to the positions of philosophers such as Stevenson and Ayer. On one hand, both Stevenson and Ayer specifically have distinguished their positions from relativism. Thus, for the most part, arguments against relativism will have no logical relation to Stevenson's and Ayer's positions. Some of them may, however, have a psychological relation.

This deserves elaboration. While no one, to my knowledge, has been perverse enough to put forward an emotive theory of philosophy, it is clearly true that extra-logical factors may affect a man's acceptance or rejection of a philosophical theory. Otherwise it would be difficult to explain how intelligent, logically equipped philosophers so regularly continue to debate among themselves the merits of (in many cases) persisting philosophical theories. Now a great many of these extra-logical factors appear to centre on the 'intuitive' appeal of competing world-views or assumptions. But in the case of ethical philosophies, ethical factors appear to have great psychological weight. Clearly there is something in the ethical climate of our time which has made Stevenson's and Ayer's ethical philosophies appear so palatable to so many people. (Had they been put forward in the seventeenth century there are many reasons, not all of them intellectual, why they would not have been widely accepted.) Arguably this feature of our ethical climate is also reflected, far more crudely, in the popularity of various forms of relativism; and the fact that it is more nakedly expressed in relativism makes it susceptible to examination by means of an examination of relativism. Thus, also, arguments against relativism, by undermining those ethical orientations which are conducive to acceptance of relativism, may have a therapeutic effect in relation to acceptance of the positions of Stevenson and Ayer.

Relativism differs in one major respect from Ayer's position and from the position that Stevenson takes in Essays 5 and 11 of *Facts and Values*. Relativists are willing to speak of ethical statements as 'true' or 'valid', not merely in a re-iterative use of 'true' or 'valid' and not merely in cases in which the statement makes a factual classification rather than a normative judgment. Relativists however always use 'true' and 'valid' in ethics in what I have called a 'qualified' sense: the ascription of truth or validity is made logically dependent on the opinion or attitude of some group of people or some individual. For relativists, in other words, ethical truth or validity is 'relative'.

In a very common form of relativism, ethical truth or validity is 'relative' to a society or culture: thus certain things which are true or valid relative to American culture are not true or valid relative to the culture of Dobu Indians, and vice versa. In another form of relativism, ethical truth or validity is relative to the individual who makes an ethical claim. Thus, if you sincerely believe that something is right, this is true relative to you, although it may not be true relative to someone else.

Relativists however are united in rejecting something which Ayer and Stevenson also reject. This is the 'absolutist' claim, implicit in the work of philosophers as diverse as Moore, Kant, Plato, and Aristotle that some ethical claims are true or valid in a way which cannot be interpreted merely in terms of description of, or logical dependence on, the attitudes or opinions of ethical agents. This is a claim which Ayer rejects as nonsense; Stevenson rejects it as a confused analysis; and relativists also reject it.

I

I shall make three points about relativism in this chapter. The first is that, despite the way it is sometimes presented, it is a philosophical position (rather than a scientific finding). The second is that the intellectual roots of its appeal are weak indeed, that it is made to seem attractive on the basis of specious premises. The third point is that the ethical roots of the appeal of relativism are specious also, and that in fact widespread acceptance of a relativist way of speaking would provide very mixed blessings.

The first point is especially necessary because so many of the popular purveyors of relativism are social scientists. It may well be that relativism had a much greater vogue among social scientists between the wars than it has now. Clyde Kluckhohn claimed in 1955 that 'Few anthropologists would today defend without important qualification Ruth Benedict's famous statement: '. . . the coexisting and equally valid patterns of life which mankind has carved for itself from the raw materials of existence'.[1] Nevertheless there are milder forms of relativism than Mrs Benedict's, and there clearly remain more than one or two social scientists who are relativists. Under their sponsorship, relativism may be presented as a scientific or quasi-scientific theory, especially if it is presented in connection with a collection of supporting facts. Thus Melville Hershkovits speaks of cultural relativism as representing 'a scientific, inductive attack on an age-old philosophical problem, using fresh, cross-cultural data, hitherto not available to scholars, gained from the study of the underlying value-systems of societies having the most diverse customs'.[2]

Relativists often appeal to anthropological facts as if these 'prove' relativism. For example, relativists are quick to point out that customs and moral judgments vary from culture to culture. Some Eskimos set their old people on ice floes, instead of sending them to old people's homes. The Dobu Indians are aggressive in a way which would shock most Americans. Relativists often point out cheerfully that there is scarcely anything of which we disapprove which is not practiced and approved in some culture in the world.

In addition some relativists point out great differences in ethical opinion even within our own culture. For example, there are sharp differences concerning the morality of war. There is not entire uniformity of moral opinion about sex, aggressive behaviour, or cheating of insurance companies. Relativists also point out that no theory of what is right and wrong has ever been proposed which could attract entire agreement within our culture, let alone entire agreement among the cultures of the world.

[1] 'Culture and Behaviour', *Collected Essays of Clyde Kluckhohn*, ed. Richard Kluckhohn (New York: The Free Press, 1962), p. 266.
[2] *Cultural Anthropology* (New York: Alfred A. Knopf, 1963), p. 351.

All of these are facts, and they are cited in support of relativism. Does this mean that relativism is an empirical, and not a philosophical, theory? To someone who is not very familiar with philosophy it might seem so. A trained philosopher, however, can recognize that the relation of relativism to facts is by no means unusual for a philosophical theory.

Take for example Bishop Berkeley's major philosophical theory, idealism. Idealism is a position in ontology which is comparable in one or two respects to relativism in ethics, although in some respects it is far from being parallel. Idealism argues that there are no objective physical objects external to minds, and that what we think of as material objects are in fact ideas in minds.

Berkeley supported this view with facts. He pointed out that the same body of (lukewarm) water can seem cool to one hand (which has been in hot water) and warm to another (which has been in cold water).[1] He pointed out that objects viewed through a microscope sometimes appear to have different colours from those which appear to the naked eye.[2] He pointed out that objects which seem one shape at a distance sometimes seem another shape close up.[3] Berkeley indeed pointed to a number of facts, all of which revealed that 'objective external realities' can seem quite different to different observers.

Because of his reliance on facts, many beginners at philosophy interpret Berkeley's thesis as empirical. A little consideration shows that it is not. There is no experiment or observation that can prove Berkeley wrong or prove him right. Any experiment, for example, which purports to show that material objects exist outside of minds can simply be interpreted by Berkeley as being really about ideas in mind. Berkeley can translate any findings about material objects into his own terms, i.e. as findings about ideas in minds.

Conversely it is quite possible to agree to all of the facts that Berkeley cites, and still deny Berkeley's position. Many philosophers indeed agree that objects can seem to observers at different distances to have different shapes, that a single body of water can seem both warm and cool, and that objects viewed through a microscope may reveal different colours from those revealed to the naked eye. They agree to these facts, but still insist that the conventions of language give us a right to describe objects as indeed

[1] 'First Dialogue Between Hylas and Philonous', in *A Theory of Vision and Other Select Philosophical Writings* (London: J. M. Dent & Sons, 1929), p. 208.
[2] *ibid.*, p. 214. [3] *ibid.*, p. 234.

having the colours that they manifest to the naked eye, the water as being really lukewarm, etc.

Let me put this another way. From the point of view of someone more concerned with language than ontology, what Berkeley really is proposing (even though he himself did not think of it entirely in this way) is a new version of English, in which all references to material objects outside of minds are replaced by references to ideas in minds. Call this Berkeley-English. The relation of facts to Berkeley's recommendation of Berkeley-English is not entirely clear, but it seems to be something like this. Berkeley feels that the facts he points to tend to be ignored by most people. He feels that when they are mentioned, they tend to be referred to in a confused, awkward manner. To holders of Berkeley's conceptions (speakers of Berkeley-English), on the other hand, these facts will seem prominent, and they will be able to be referred to in a graceful manner. Many other philosophers, however, have not felt that Berkeley's facts are so important, or are so poorly dealt with in ordinary English, that we require a new version of English to accommodate them.

Very similar points can be made about the relation of relativism to facts. Even though relativists support their views with facts, there is no empirical way to prove or to disprove relativism. After all, any facts about the diversity of moral opinions can be accommodated by an anti-relativist. He may simply say 'Here are more instances of some people being right in ethical matters and of other people being wrong'. On the other hand, if there were sudden complete agreement among the people of the world as to moral matters, this would not prove relativism wrong. The relativist could still argue that *if* two cultures disagreed as to the morality of an action, we would never be entitled to say that one was right and the other was wrong.

A theory which is consistent with all possible collections of facts is not empirical. Neither relativism nor the denial of relativism is empirical. Neither would be seriously affected by, for example, new anthropological discoveries. In particular, relativism is not refuted (although it may be undermined) by social scientific claims to have demonstrated the 'existence of universal values' at the 'conceptual' level.[1]

[1] Cf. Ralph Linton, 'The Problem of Universal Values', *Method and Perspective in Anthropology, Papers in Honor of Wilson D. Wallis*, ed. Robert F. Spencer (Minneapolis: University of Minnesota Press, 1954).

Relativism is usually presented as part of a package which includes facts, but actually it is designed to provide a way of putting facts. The facts of moral diversity are widely acknowledged even by anti-relativists; but the relativist wishes to do more than merely report these facts. He wishes to present them *in a certain way*. Instead of merely saying 'Here are instances of moral diversity among cultures', he wishes to say 'Here are examples of how there is no right or wrong apart from the standards of a particular culture or individual'. That is, the relativist wishes to put a philosophical gloss on the facts. The facts are empirical; relativism is the philosophical gloss.

II

Let me elaborate on one parallel between relativism and Berkeley's idealism. This is that both involve a sharp departure from ordinary English. Both in effect propose a new language which is partly based on familiar English.

This can be seen quite clearly in the case of Berkeley's idealism. Ordinary English does not allow us to speak of a table as being equivalent to ideas in the mind. The ordinary translation of 'There is a table next to me' is not anything like 'I have an idea of a table next to me (and if I do not, at least God has)'. The ordinary meaning would be more like 'Even if I did not think that there were, and even if God did not exist, there would be a real material table next to me.' Statements about tables and chairs are normally discussed in a language replete with the terminology of the material world: ultimately to disallow this terminology, and to suggest that the terminology of the mental world is the only appropriate one, is to substitute a new (but related) language for ordinary English.

Similarly, ordinary English does not allow us to speak of the goodness of a thing as simply a function of opinions or attitudes. The ordinary translation of 'X is good' is not anything like 'I (or my society) approve of X'. The ordinary meaning would be more like 'Even if my society and I did not approve of X, X still would be good'. Statements about goodness and obligation are normally discussed in a language replete with terminology implying that there are ethically correct or incorrect statements, apart from what people may happen to think. Ultimately to disallow this terminology, and to suggest that the terminology of opinion, approval, or disapproval can provide the substance of ethics, is to substitute a new (but related) language for ordinary English.

We may ask, then, 'Why make this substitution?' What are the advantages of a relativist way of speech supposed to be; what is its appeal? The answer is that relativism has two major attractions, one intellectual and one ethical. The ethical attraction is undoubtedly the greater, and it is the one which I shall discuss at greater length. First, however, I shall survey the intellectual attraction.

The intellectual attraction of relativism is very similar to one of the attractions of Berkeley's idealism. It is that relativism, like idealism, gives the appearance of resolutely sticking to what we are entitled to say. Many people are very concerned to avoid the risk of error, and 'not to go beyond the facts'. Both relativism and idealism have a strong appeal for such people.

Some of this can be seen in reasons which are sometimes given for endorsing idealism. All that we really know, it is pointed out, consists of our experiences, i.e. contents of our minds. The inferences from these experiences to physical objects outside of our minds are dubious. They cannot be rationally justified.

Not only are the inferences from experiences to independent physical objects said to be dubious, but also they are said to lead to an unintelligible conclusion. It is argued that we have no clear conception of material substance outside of the mind. All that we can conceive of is based on what we have experienced, and all that we have experienced is within the mind. Thus non-mental substance is unintelligible as well as unprovable.

This is a very appealing argument. How much better and more secure it is to reject unprovable and mysterious claims! Philosophers who restrict their ontology to things which we assuredly know, appear to be the most hard-headed. On the basis of the argument that all that we directly know is the contents of our minds, idealism would appear to be the most hard-headed and secure philosophy.

There is no need to go into arguments against this. A number of philosophers have shot holes into the argument that we somehow have more dependable acquaintance with minds than we do with physical objects. Analysis of the meaning of words referring to physical objects has put the whole issue in a new light.[1]

What I want to point out simply is that some of the intellectual appeal of relativism is similar to that enjoyed by idealism. The

[1] See for example A. J. Ayer, *The Problem of Knowledge* (Harmondsworth: Penguin Books, 1956), Chapter III.

similarity is not extremely close. For one thing, there are arguments in support of idealism far more complex than the one that I have outlined here. Some aspects of the appeals of idealism and relativism are very dissimilar. Nevertheless, a good deal of the appeal of idealism is found in the simple argument which I gave; and relativism does appeal to people in a similar way. It too, claims to stick to what we are clearly entitled to say. It too, rejects unprovable and mysterious claims.

Relativists often argue, for example, that all that we really are entitled to say is that some cultures believe that certain things are right, and other cultures believe that other things are right. If we stick to the facts, they suggest, we are intellectually secure. We lose this security, on the other hand, if we start making judgments that certain things really *are* right.

Judgments that certain things really are right have serious drawbacks. First of all, they can never be proved. Relativists often point out how even very obvious-sounding ethical propositions are disputed in some part of the world. They also point out that no philosopher has ever succeeded in finding 'self-evident' ethical principles that would be accepted by all other philosophers. 'Each founder of a new theory hopes that it is he who has discovered the unique jewel of moral truth . .'.[1] But such hopes, the argument runs, are doomed to disappointment.

Relativists also argue that judgments that something is 'really right' (or 'really good') lack clear meaning. They point out that it is quite clear what is meant when the moral opinions of various people are described. What are described are observable phenomena. But for something to be 'really right' or 'really good' seems quite different. What do these terms mean?

Relativists, in other words, have some of the same difficulty with the concept of being really right (or being really good) that Berkeley had with the concept of independently existing material objects. They cannot make out what it would be for something to be really right. Berkeley argued that we are directly acquainted only with experiences of objects, and never with independently existing material objects. In the same way, relativists argue that we are acquainted only with ethical opinions and attitudes, and never with goodness, rightness, etc.

Let me, as a consequence of my previous observations, point out

[1] Edward Westermarck, *Ethical Relativity* (Patterson, New Jersey: Littlefield, Adams & Co., 1960), p. 4.

a dilemma for the relativist. Either the argument I have just out-lined rests on a covert simplification and modification of ordinary language, or (if it pretends to be valid within the framework of ordinary language) it rests on at least two serious confusions.

The first confusion involves ignoring a basic distinction in the workings of language. This is between, on one hand, what we can be sure about in relation to a statement, and, on the other hand, what the statement claims. Awareness of this distinction vitiates any argument that, because we cannot prove claims that something is really right (independently of what attitudes or opinions happen to be), we are not really making these claims.

Actually this distinction is very important with regard to almost all of our claims to knowledge. Let us suppose that we reject proofs for commonsense beliefs, such as those Descartes offers. We then appear to be left with the realization that we believe, and claim, a great many things which we cannot prove. Indeed it appears that we believe and claim a great many things for which we never will have very conclusive evidence. Some people cannot accept this con-clusion. They cannot accept the idea that our claims go beyond what we are assured of.

A way that is often suggested of escaping the conclusion is this. What we seem to claim, it is said, is not really what we claim. We seem to claim all sorts of things that go beyond the evidence, but actually our claims are simply equivalent to a statement of the evidence that we have. Thus we do not really make unprovable claims.

This way of escape has been suggested by some philosophers of science, who argued that scientific theories are just restatements of the data. When a relativist insists that ethical statements actually do not claim more than would be claimed by a description of ethical opinions and attitudes, he is making in some respects a similar move. He is trying to squeeze what is claimed into the dimensions of what we are assured of.

Once we have a clear awareness of the workings of language, however, we realize the inadequacy of this. We realize that what we claim very frequently exceeds what we are entitled to be sure of. In the light of this, unless we reject ordinary language it is fallacious to argue that because we cannot prove that certain things are 'really right' (or 'really good') we can, in fact, never claim that certain things are really right or good.

If a relativist becomes convinced that we sometimes really are claiming that certain things really are right or good, he may take another tack. The argument then may become that a claim of real rightness or goodness, if it is interpreted as going beyond a description of ethical opinion or attitude, lacks meaning. It lacks meaning because the notion of real rightness or goodness, independent of what people think is right or good, is unintelligible. After all, can we point to real goodness or real rightness?

Given the framework of ordinary language, we can see that this confusion is embodied in the well-worn theory that all meaning is built into what we are directly acquainted with, and that words straightforwardly take their meaning from what they correspond to. This theory was widely held in the earlier part of this century. Moore was, as I have pointed out, not entirely free from its influence. But Wittgenstein's *Philosophical Investigations* laid it to rest, and very few philosophers would defend it now.

It has been common among followers of Wittgenstein to say 'The meaning is the use'. Applying this idea, we see that it is fallacious to conclude that, just because we cannot point to any entity which would be called real goodness, statements such as 'X is good, quite apart from what I or my cultural group think' lack meaning. After all, such statements have a use. Relativists themselves know how to use them, if they can overcome their inhibitions. This shows that, despite what they say, they know the meanings of claims that something is 'really good' or 'really right'.

Thus either the intellectual appeal of relativism involves the covert rejection of ordinary language, or it is based on some fairly simple confusions about language. I have indicated, however, that the popularity of relativism is caused more by an ethical appeal than by an intellectual appeal. We can now examine this ethical appeal.

III

The major appeal of relativism must be put into the context of a reaction against the excesses of the nineteenth century. It is now widely accepted that many nineteenth-century thinkers were rigid and dogmatic on moral questions. The ordinary righteous nineteenth century European or American was also often rigid. When he encountered people of other cultures, especially primitive cultures, he often did not make allowances for the differences between their habits and circumstances and his own. He often judged them as if they were Europeans or Americans. He assumed, that is, that the standards of his society were correct and fully applicable. By these standards the people of primitive cultures were inferior, and often had to be classified as reprobates.

The result in many cases was an intolerable excess of interference. Often viable traditional cultures were thoroughly disrupted. It goes without saying that members of these culture groups were not immediately transformed into Europeans or Americans. Quite often they sank into a way of life which was in many respects inferior to the life they led before the interference began.

Thus it can be argued, and indeed appears to be true, that a prevalent belief in the superiority of modern Western culture was intimately connected with some unfortunate policies. As Hershkovits puts it, 'It is when, as in Euro-American culture, ethnocentrism is rationalized and made the basis of programmes of action detrimental to the well-being of other peoples that it gives rise to serious problems.'[1] This 'ethnocentrism' might be argued to be a combination of two factors: 'absolutism' in ethics (the belief that something may be right or wrong independently of what any culture or individual happens to believe), plus the belief that in fact one's own culture has arrived at the correct answers.

All of this provides relativism with considerable ethical appeal. 'Absolutism', it is said, has led, and still leads, to intolerance. Relativism promotes tolerance. Therefore we all should be relativists.

This is a very appealing argument. As D. H. Munro has said, 'Many people are attracted to relativism because they prefer the attitude of the anthropologist to that of the missionary.'[2] Nevertheless Munro has argued that 'Tolerance does not really follow from relativism.'[3] There is no logical inconsistency in a relativist's violently pursuing the values which he judges correct relative to *his* opinions, and violently condemning values which he judges incorrect relative to his opinions.

That there is indeed a connection between relativism and tolerance may be (and has been) argued as follows. Relativists urge us not to speak of practices as really right or really wrong, but instead to speak of practices as right or wrong relative to a culture (or to an individual). Presumably then, instead of worrying about whether certain primitive customs are really right or really wrong, we will

[1] *op. cit.*, p. 356.
[2] *Empiricism and Ethics* (London: Cambridge University Press, 1967), p. 114.
[3] *loc. cit.*

be able quite cheerfully to say 'They are right relative to these people'. If we speak this way, there may be no logical reason which is guaranteed to prevent us from pursuing our own values single-mindedly, at the expense of everyone else's. But relativists suggest that the general effect of recognizing that other people's ethical judgments are right relative to them or their culture will normally be one of softening our opposition to these judgments. By appreciating their point of view better, we ought to accommodate to it better. Thus relativists claim that relativism, while it may not entail tolerance, can be expected to promote it.

I may say that I agree with this. It must be conceded that there are fewer intolerant relativists than there are intolerant people who speak about ethical questions in the ordinary way, and that this is a natural outcome of relativism. Since we all nowadays, very broadly speaking, favour tolerance, it may seem indeed to follow from this that it is quite desirable to change from what at present is ordinary English to a relativist mode of speech. However, I shall urge two objections. One is that a relativist way of speaking is by no means required to be tolerant. The other is that someone who thoroughly accepts relativism will thereby be encouraged to be tolerant to a fault.

First, we do not have to accept the relativist thesis in order to recognize that certain courses of action which are justified in the setting of one culture are not justified in the setting of another culture. The point may be illustrated as follows.

Suppose that we accept the utilitarian principle that the best action to perform is one which has the best total consequences. We can recognize that the consequences to be weighed in, for example, deciding to set old people on ice floes, were different in Eskimo society than they would be in America. Not setting the old people on ice floes would have had different consequences, in terms of food shortages, in Eskimo society than it would in America.

It would not follow from this that setting old people on ice floes was right for Eskimos. But it does follow that the decision of whether the Eskimos were right to send their old people to their deaths is quite a separate decision from that of whether we in America would be justified in doing the same thing. If the consequences of keeping the old people alive were really drastically different in Eskimo society than they would be in America, it is at least conceivable that some unprejudiced observers might conclude that what the Eskimos did was for the best.

In other words, someone who applies the utilitarian principle can conclude that certain practices which are right in the context of one culture would be wrong in the context of another. What is for the best in America might not be for the best in the circumstances of New Guinea, and vice versa. Indeed only an excessively rigid person would refuse to recognize this. Only an excessively rigid person would refuse to consider a variation in circumstances when he was judging the appropriateness of an action.

It is by no means the case, however, that someone who adopts this line of thought is committed to relativism. For one thing, there is a major gulf between saying that *some* actions which are wrong within the context of one culture are right within the context of another culture, and saying that all ethical rightness is relative. For another thing, there is a major difference between saying that the rightness of an action may depend in part on circumstances, and saying that rightness and wrongness are simply a function of the opinions of a culture or an individual.

Thus, if we accept the utilitarian principle, we are not required to accept the views of a culture as to what is right or wrong in the circumstances to be found in that culture. We need not conclude that setting old people on ice floes was right within a given Eskimo tribe, even if the whole tribe traditionally believed so. Whether it was right depended on whether the consequences were the best, and it could be that the whole tribe had shortsightedly misjudged this.

There are some actions so extreme that it is hard to imagine circumstances in which they would have better consequences than their alternatives would. Torture is one example. Murder of innocent people (e.g. by head-hunters) when there is no acute food shortage is another. Even if a whole culture were to judge these actions right, we would not be committed by the utilitarian principle to ratify their judgment. We would be quite free to point out that these actions were wrong.

In the case of many tribal customs, though, someone who adopts the utilitarian principle will be cautious in judging. He will recognize that many customs of a primitive people are so closely related to the general fabric of the culture that one cannot attack a custom without undermining the whole culture. He will recognize also that it is not easy for a people whose culture has been undermined to adapt to new viable ways.

Thus someone need not be a relativist in order to be very cautious in judging other cultures. We do not have to be relativists in order to be tolerant of strange customs, even if they seem at first to be highly distasteful.

Also, someone does not have to be a relativist in order to have a civilized disinclination to interfere in other people's business. The people who interfered in primitive cultures, and disoriented their people, were in many cases simply busybodies. Really civilized people, whether they are relativists or not, generally do not act like this. They generally do not make reforming others the major business of their lives. Even within our own society, we normally do not tell people exactly what we think of them. When we see a man making a mess of his life, in most circumstances we consider it ordinary prudence not to try to manage him.

In other words, civilized restraint is at least as reliable as relativism in preventing unwarranted interference with the lives of primitive peoples. I am also prepared to argue that civilized restraint can promote tolerance more selectively than relativism. The tolerance that I have been advocating has its limits. There are some cases in which even a highly civilized person will actively interfere in the life of another. We feel usually that we ought to interfere when someone attempts suicide, for example. We also ought to interfere when it is extremely clear that we can do some good without undermining the independence of the person we help. Similarly, there arguably are cases in which customs of a primitive people should be attacked. It is quite arguable, for example, that the Australian government is justified in attempting to curb head-hunting among natives in New Guinea. Quite clearly, there can be cases in which a custom is so destructive that the good effects of removing it outweigh the bad effects of disturbing the culture.

There is nothing logically which prevents a relativist from acknowledging this (relative to his own values, of course), but the softening of our opposition to the values of other cultures which relativism accomplishes is a *general* softening; and consequently many relativists appear not to be selective in their tolerance. After all, the relativist position forces one to speak of *all* customs as right relative to the opinions of the people who think them right. This applies to head-hunting as well as polygamy; it also presumably applies to the practices of the Nazis as well as of the Samoans. One can still declare some of these practices to be wrong relative to one's own values, but having admitted them to be right relative to the people who pursue them does blunt the edge of moral criticism.

The general softening of moral opposition to the practices of other people which accompanies relativism sometimes can lead to a ridiculous refusal to say the obvious. Take for example the case of the Dobu Indians of Melanesia. Their culture, as it is described by Ruth Benedict in *Patterns of Culture*, is obviously one of the least satisfactory ones the world has seen. To say this, does not convict us of being 'culture bound', or of being sunk in 'the ethnocentric morass in which our thinking about ultimate values has for so long bogged down'.[1] We can appreciate some of the tremendous virtues of, say Japanese culture, or of ancient Iranian culture. We can judge some cultures other than our own to have great merits, and to be superior to our own in many respects. Equally we can judge the Dobu culture to have very great faults, and to have few compensating advantages.

The Dobus, as Mrs Benedict describes them, are habitually in a semi-paranoiac state. Their culture makes them suspicious and hostile to those around them. The culture encourages aggressive behaviour. Furthermore, as she points out, the culture does not provide the possibility of those creative outlets which advanced cultures generally allow; e.g. 'a talent for observation expends itself in some Melanesian tribe upon the negligible borders of the magico-religious field'.[2]

In the light of this, it seems odd that Mrs Benedict made her famous statement that various cultures, the Dobu included, are 'coexisting and equally valid patterns of life which mankind has created for itself from the raw materials of existence'.[3] Quite clearly the Dobu culture is inferior. Then why not say it? Only someone whose mind was wedded to a theory would thus inhibit herself. But when a theory leads to absurdities, it ought to be abandoned.

I should point out that Mrs Benedict's statement is not a logical consequence of relativism, but represents a further step. The relativist of course is free to say that, relative to his values, not all cultures are 'equally valid'. But it is clear that relativism often leads, as in Mrs Benedict's case, to the presumption of equality among cultures. It also is clear why. If we reject 'absolutist' attempts to determine which practices are really right, then with regard to these traditional judgments all cultures are on a par. They are equal at least in not being able to be judged by 'absolutist'

[1] Hershkovits, *op. cit.*, p. 366.
[2] *Patterns of Culture* (New York: Mentor Books, 1960), pp. 218–19.
[3] *ibid.*, p. 240.

standards. It is a short step from this to the claim that cultures are equal in not being able to be judged by standards outside of themselves (the move to legislate ethical tolerance). It then becomes tempting to summarize this by saying simply that all cultures are equal.

All of this I think documents my charge that relativism encourages people to be tolerant to a fault. It may be objected that after all a relativist need not be tolerant to a fault. But I have argued that someone who opposes relativism need not be intolerant, and also of course need not be tolerant to a fault. So where does the advantage of relativism lie? What reason can be given for changing our way of speaking to a relativist mode? There appears to be no good reason.

Having said this, I must make an important admission. It is that our way of speaking does appear, at least to some degree, to be changing. It is clear that in the contemporary climate of ethical opinion there is considerable sympathy for the extreme tolerance that relativism is recognized as promoting, and considerable sympathy for relativism. This inevitably must affect ways of using ethical language. I would argue that thusfar the effects have been quite superficial: people who are sympathetic to relativism use relativistic ways of talking when the point is at issue, and then on the street lapse into traditional uses of ethical language. But it is not inconceivable that the time will come when the dominant patterns of ethical discourse will be relativistic.

Two points should be made about this. One is that this eventuality is very far from certain, and would be extremely undesirable. Clyde Kluckhohn says that

'One of the broadest and surest generalizations that anthropology can make about human beings is that no society is healthy or creative or strong unless that society has a set of common values that give meaning and purpose to group life, that can be symbolically expressed, that fit with the situation of the time as well as being linked to the historical past, and that do not outrage men's reason and at the same time appeal to their emotions.'[1]

It is debatable whether it is possible for a society to cherish a set of common values to the extent that they 'give meaning and purpose to group life' without at the same time firmly rejecting some alternative

[1] 'Culture and Behaviour', *Collected Essays of Clyde Kluckhohn*, ed. Richard Kluckhohn (New York: The Free Press, 1962), pp. 297–8.

sets of values. If we remain very aware of the acceptance elsewhere of values which are traditionally repugnant to our society, and if relativism promotes a softening of our rejection of these values, then to that extent we arguably are moving further from the conditions for a healthy society which Kluckhohn sketches.

The second point is that if the dominant patterns of ethical discourse ever did become relativistic, then the burden of argument would be on the anti-relativist: he would have to argue that there are overriding ethical or philosophical reasons for the rejection of relativism. I have given ample indication, I hope, that these reasons could be produced. Under the present conditions of our ordinary ethical discourse, however, the burden of argument is on the relativist. He must show overriding reasons for adopting a relativistic way of talking. I have argued that the philosophical arguments for relativism are specious, and that the ethical advantages claimed for a relativistic way of talking are balanced by disadvantages and could be gained in other ways.

PART II

THE EXISTENCE
OF ETHICAL KNOWLEDGE

CHAPTER VI
EXPERIENCE IN ETHICS

Aristotle says that we ought to pay much attention to older men, 'for experience has given such men an eye with which they can see correctly'.[1] In this chapter we shall inquire how experience may promote this ethical intelligence, and more broadly into the role experience plays in ethics.

A number of purposes will be accomplished by this discussion. First, since experience is so widely recognized as playing a cognitive role in the sciences, exposing the role of experience in ethics should contribute to the case for saying that there is ethical knowledge. This chapter is the first step in building this case. Secondly, comparison of experience in ethics with experience in the sciences helps to underline the narrowness of the criteria for literal meaning which Ayer applies to ethics. Thirdly, this discussion hopefully will help to expose the one-sidedness of much very recent work in ethics (some of which will be discussed in Chapter VII). Many writers have concentrated on pointing out the respects in which reason plays an important role in ethics. This represents a healthy reaction against emotivist theories, but centres the cognitive nature of ethics too much on arguments and inference. This chapter will point out some of what they have been neglecting.

I

I shall begin by giving some examples of ethical judgments at which people might claim to have arrived as a result of experience. We then can examine whether these claims can be justified, and we can ask whether ethical experience in some cases may confer a 'right to be confident'. Then we can ask what the nature of ethical experience is.

Example 1. A is a policeman who has worked for many years with juvenile offenders. He has noticed that juvenile offenders who commit crimes for which they will easily be caught usually have emotional problems, and usually do not repeat offences. He says of one such offender, 'He is not so bad.'

[1] *Nichomachean Ethics*, trans. Martin Ostwald (New York: Library of Liberal Arts, 1962), p. 167.

Example 2. B's major ambition is to be wealthy and famous. He is privileged to spend a weekend at the home of Mr X who is very wealthy and very famous, and cares deeply about his wealth and reputation. During the weekend, he notices the boring nature of many of Mr X's obligations, the superficial relations Mr X has with his family, the mask-like expression on Mr X's face at certain moments. At the end of the weekend, he says that he has seen the emptiness and undesirability of a life centred around wealth and fame.

Example 3. C robs a shopkeeper of his savings, and is not apprehended. Later he has the opportunity to observe the effects of his theft on the unfortunate shopkeeper, who has become extremely depressed, and begins to neglect the routines of his work. Eventually C says that he sees that what he did was wrong.

Example 4. Sartre describes an occasion on which one of his pupils had to choose between staying at home with his dependent mother, and attempting to go to England to join the Free French.[1] Let us imagine D in a situation like this, and suppose that D has seen a friend who remained with his mother become increasingly depressed and ineffectual. He also has seen himself become sullen and resentful under constraint enough times to know that he probably, if he remained with his mother, would come to resent her and treat her badly. Let us suppose that D then decides that it would be better for him to attempt to go to England.

Now it is clear that in each of these cases the ethical judgment *could* have been made without the benefit of the related experience. Any inexperienced person can judge that a juvenile offender is 'not so bad'. Anyone can judge that a life centred around wealth and fame is empty, even without the benefit of a weekend at the home of a wealthy, famous man who cares deeply about wealth and fame. Most of us consider stealing wrong, even if we have not closely observed the effects of a theft on its victim. Some people, also, would say that anyone in a situation like that of Sartre's pupil ought to leave home, and would say this even without the benefit of experience of cases of this type.

[1] Cf. 'Existentialism is a Humanism', included in Morton White, *The Age of Analysis* (New York: Mentor Books, 1955). Problems surrounding Sartre's example are dealt with at considerable length in my essay 'Nuance and Ethical Choice', *Ethics*, January 1969.

It further is clear that someone could be confronted by the events by which A, B, C, and D are confronted, and yet not come to their conclusions. A fellow policeman may differ with A's evaluation of the juvenile offender; another ambitious young man may conclude a weekend at Mr X's with even greater enthusiasm for a life centred on wealth and fame; another thief may, after seeing the sufferings of one of his victims, still feel that what he did was somehow justified; and D does not have to decide as he does. (It is of course questionable whether being confronted with the same events is tantamount to having the same experiences: this is a topic which we shall take up later.)

Even if experience is not required to arrive at any given ethical judgment, and perhaps need not be decisive, it may be decisive. It is very easy to suppose that A would not have arrived at his judgment of the juvenile offender were it not for his experience, that B would continue to value wealth and fame very highly were it not for what he saw, that C would not have repented were it not for his experience, and that D would have judged his situation differently were it not for his experience. Not all ethical judgments are made directly on the basis of experience, but many are.

This much is obvious. We may ask now about a more difficult matter: whether ethical experience in some cases confers a 'right to be confident'. This is a complex question. The right to be confident admits of degrees. The right to be confident which one may have *without* experience (e.g. if one relies on authority) varies with the case. Furthermore, whether someone has the right to be confident of an ethical judgment clearly may be as controversial as whether the judgment itself is correct.

Example 3 is at one extreme in all of these respects. There is little controversy in our society at the moment about whether theft (at least in cases in which there are no special exculpating factors) is wrong. It is generally agreed that the majority of people know that theft is wrong. Furthermore the view that theft is wrong is so thoroughly traditional that adults of normal intelligence are widely accorded the right to be thoroughly confident of a judgment made purely on the basis of authority. Not many people would hold that C's experience gave him a much greater than normal right to be confident that theft is wrong, simply because the normal right is considered so great.

The major function of experience in a case like that of Example 3 is to make us more aware of what we ought already to know.

Immoral behaviour is often in part a result of insensitivity: the immoral person oftens knows (at least in broad outline) the effects of his actions, but may manage not to think about them, or not to notice them. Arguably there would be appreciably less behaviour harmful to other people if everyone were forced to mark in detail the results of his actions. Experience, in cases like that of Example 3, does not so much contribute extra elements to the case supporting an ethical judgment as it does bring the case into focus.

Example 2 lies toward the other extreme from Example 3. There is a good deal of controversy in our society concerning the real value of such things as wealth and fame. B's judgment would not find the same degree of consensus as C's. Indeed the claim that B has the same right to be confident as C would not be very widely agreed to: even people who agreed with B's judgment might feel that one did not have the same right to be confident of a judgment with which reputable men differed as one had to be confident of a judgment which was accepted by all good citizens. Someone who made the same judgment as B, simply on the basis of authority, would be accorded by many people even less right to be confident than B: where authority is widely disputed, the right to be confident which it confers appears tenuous.

On the other hand, someone who strongly believes that B's judgment is correct may well accord B a strong right to be confident of his judgment. It would not be unusual, or odd-sounding, to speak of B as 'knowing from experience' that a life centred around wealth and fame was of little value. We might especially speak this way if B had actually lived such a life, and then rejected it. We might then well say of B's value judgment, 'He ought to know'; although of course we would be unlikely to say this unless we tended to agree with B's judgment.

Even if we accorded B a strong right to be confident of his judgment, we would be unlikely to accord anything like the same right to someone who made B's judgment on the basis of authority (even if it is on the basis of B's authority). We would not say that such a person 'ought to know'. The perfectly natural challenge, 'How do you know that a life centred on wealth and fame is not highly desirable?' which B can satisfy by saying, 'I have seen . . .', could not be satisfied nearly as well by saying, 'I have been told . . .'.

Many people feel that they gain from novels and plays insights of the character which B claims that he gained from experience. Many people claim that they can arrive at value judgments of ways of life by imaginatively 'trying them out', and that literary works help them in this. There do seem to be novels, such as *Rasselas* and *Candide*, which are devoted in large part to this purpose. Many writers, most notably I. A. Richards in *Principles of Literary Criticism*, have been impressed by the influence of literature upon our responses to problems which we encounter in our lives. Novels and plays clearly do *suggest* a great deal, as well perhaps as structuring our responses. But most of us would, on reflection, consider novels and plays less reliable than lived experience. If B is asked 'How do you know that a life centred on wealth and fame is not highly desirable?' 'From the way it was portrayed in a novel' is not as satisfactory a reply as 'I have seen . . .', even if the novel is indeed a very good novel.

One of the advantages that someone who had observed at close hand a life centred on wealth and fame has over someone who merely has read about such a life is simply that the man with experience can claim to know what he is judging. He can claim to 'know what it is like'. This does not ensure the correctness of his judgment; and, for that matter, there is no guarantee that he really has perceived adequately what he judges. But at the very least he has been in the right position, and thus has much the same advantage over the novel-reader that a witness to a crime has over the man who merely reads about it in the newspapers.

That experience may confer an increased right to be confident of an ethical judgment is perhaps most clear *vis-à-vis* Examples 1 and 4. One reason for this is that the judgments made in these two cases, although they are ethical judgments, are intimately related to predictions. A in effect predicts that the juvenile offender will not continue to behave very badly; D predicts that on the balance there will be less unhappiness and bitterness if he leaves home. The predictions of both A and D are related to their having seen the workings out of relevant causal patterns.

It is worth pointing out that judgments of character almost always involve a predictive or counterfactual element. A major exception might be claimed to be judgments of the character of men who are dead or dying; but arguably even here counterfactuals (what a man would have done if such and such had happened) play an important role in the assessment of the motives which lay behind actions. It clearly is true in the cases of people who are still very much alive that what one judges in their character is to a great degree dispositions. Honesty, temperance, intelligence, and loyalty are all dispositional: to judge them is in large part to judge how a man will, or would, act in certain circumstances. (To say this is not to succumb to the 'naturalistic fallacy': it is possible, although not very common, for two people to agree in their judgments of what a man would have done in various circumstances, and yet to disagree in their evaluation both of his behaviour and of his character. Most commonly, however, disagreements in evaluation of a man's character are accompanied by disagreements concerning what could be expected of him.) It is widely acknowledged that relevant experience may confer a right to be confident of predictive or counterfactual judgments; so it stands to reason that the experience of A, who is in effect predicting the behaviour of the juvenile offender in relation to a standard which A assumes, confers on him a right to be confident of his ethical judgment which he would not have if the judgment did not rest on experience.

Indeed we commonly do speak of 'experienced judges of character'. Now it might be objected that we can distinguish between two performances on A's part, a predictive and an evaluative performance, and that in fact the expertise which A's experience confers on him is entirely in relation to the predictive performance, and not in relation to the evaluative performance. There is nothing wrong in breaking what A does into two stages like this: a predictive and then an evaluative stage. But it must be recognized that the second stage depends on the first. A evaluates as he does because of his predictions. Any expertise that he has at predicting also means that he has more of a basis for his evaluations than would someone who predicted poorly.

Of course we are free both to accept A's predictions and to reject his evaluations. If we do this, we may well claim that A's evaluative tendencies disqualify his claim to be confident of his evaluations: we are in an especially strong position to do this if we can show that A is bigoted, or excessively harsh, or biased against children who read books, etc. But the point remains that there is a claim to be disqualified: that A's predictive abilities give him, *prima facie*, more of a right to be confident of his evaluations than someone who lacked these predictive abilities would have. To the extent then that A's experience enables him to predict better, A's experience gives him, all things equal, more of a right to be confident of his evaluations. If A is asked 'How do you know that this juvenile offender is not so bad?' it would normally be considered perfectly adequate for him to say 'I have seen many boys of this kind . . .'.

The case of D is complicated by the fact that part of what D is predicting is his own behaviour. It can be questioned whether prediction of one's own behaviour involves cognition in the same way as prediction of other people's behaviour. Sartre at one time (when he wrote *Being and Nothingness*) appeared ready to argue that prediction of one's own behaviour simply involves decision, and that to regard it any other way is to be guilty of bad faith. This is quite plausible if the behaviour in question is an immediate and simple act (Shall I or shall I not mail this letter?). It is much less plausible in relation to complicated behaviour over a long time which involves responses which most of us would consider somewhat inadvertent. It makes much more sense for D to speculate over whether he will become irritated with his mother if he remains at home than it would be for him to speculate over whether he will now mail a letter.

It seems plausible to say that some people are much better than others at predicting their own responses, and that this is a large part of what is commonly meant by 'self-knowledge'. Self-knowledge clearly is important in ethics, to the extent that judging what way of life is most desirable for oneself is partly a matter of judging one's capabilities and tendencies, and also to the extent that one's responses are part of the consequences of one's actions. Raskolnikov, in Dostoevsky's *Crime and Punishment*, if he thought that he would retain any peace of mind after killing the old pawnbroker was deficient in self-knowledge (as well as being deficient in sensitivity to other factors in his choice); D too would be deficient in self-knowledge if he expected that he would remain a cheerful and loving son if he stayed at home.

Again, none of this is to succumb to the naturalistic fallacy. I am not suggesting that a prediction of the results of an action entails a judgment of its rightness. Two people may agree on a prediction of the results of an action, and yet differ in their evaluation of these results. Also D, if he subscribes to a deontological type of ethics, may judge that it would produce great unhappiness for everyone if he remained at home, and yet, without flatly contradicting himself, judge also that he ought to remain at home. This is unreasonable, but it is hard to argue that it can be *proved* wrong.

But if we ask D 'How do you know that you ought to leave home?' it is perfectly in order for him to reply 'I have seen myself chafe under constraint, and I anticipate that if I remained at home my behaviour would be such as to have unfortunate consequences.'

Again, both D's prediction and his judgment of what he ought to do may be incorrect. But at least he is in a position to know how he probably will behave, and to this extent I think that it would be generally conceded that D's experience gives him a greater right to be confident of his ethical judgment than he would have if he had never noticed any pattern in his own responses.

Let me sum up the argument thus far. Experience sometimes plays a decisive role in arriving at an ethical judgment. In some cases, related to familiar maxims, experience merely brings into focus what we ought already to know. In other cases, such as those of A, B, and D, I have argued that experience may put us in a specially qualified position to make an ethical judgment. Almost everyone would concede this to A, and I should think that many people would concede this to D and B. Whether one does, finally, allow a special right to be confident of their ethical judgments to A, B, and D depends to a great extent on whether one trusts their perceptions and their values, which in turn depends to a great extent on whether one is inclined to agree with their judgments. A somewhat analogous case might be that of a close witness to a crime (or the man who was standing right next to where the supposed goldfinch appeared), to whom we accord a special right to be confident of his account if we regard him as reasonably observant: whether we consider him reasonably observant depends in turn on the indications provided by whatever outside evidence we can relate to the reports he gives.

The fact remains, of course, that there are special problems in ethics for which there is nothing entirely comparable outside of ethics. The witnesses to a crime may well disagree, but we usually may hope in the end to produce some agreement concerning what happened; and of course there always is the possibility of photographs being taken of the event. But if the other guests at Mr X's home have a different impression from B's of the character of Mr X's life, normally we have less hope of resolving differences; and normally a photograph, or a motion picture, will not be decisive. The striking thing is that B and the other guests may claim to have perceived quite different things, in ways which often are difficult to account for in terms of poor eyesight, carelessness, or inattentiveness. It may be that neither the other guests nor B will ever be convinced of having made a mistake. This can happen too with regard to the conflicting accounts given by witnesses to a crime, but it is less likely.

One point which this suggests is that what in ordinary English is called 'experience' is quite complicated and diverse. Philosophers who have pointed out the diversity of 'reason' have not given similar attention to 'experience'. 'Experience' in the laboratory may have a different character, and play a different logical role, from 'experience' at the scene of a crime. B's 'experience' has a different character, and plays a different logical role, from either; it even differs significantly in character from the 'experience' of A. In what follows I shall discuss the nature of ethical 'experience'. I shall pay primary attention to the nature of B's experience, but also shall make comments about the experience of A, C, and D.

II

A good deal of what I wish to explore here has been suggested by Stuart Hampshire. He has pointed out that

'The situations in which we must act or abstain from acting, are "open" in the sense that they cannot be uniquely described and finally circumscribed. . . . Situations do not present themselves with their labels attached to them; . . . the crux is in the labelling, or the decision depends on how we see the situation.'[1]

This is true, of course, not only of situations (such as D's) in which ethical judgment may have an immediate and intimate connection with action, but also of situations (such as B's) in which ethical judgment has a much less immediate, and much more general, relation to action.

Let us suppose that G has been a weekend guest at the home of Mr X along with B, and that G arrives at a different ethical conclusion. In so far as Mr X's life may be considered typical, G judges that a life centred upon wealth and fame is rather desirable. G has, in a sense, seen the same things as B: he has been in the same rooms at the same times. But his experience leads him to an opposite ethical judgment.

Now it is possible that G and B, despite their opposing evaluations, might give the same account of what they saw. It is possible, that is, that G too might speak of the boring nature of many of Mr X's obligations, the superficial relations between Mr X and his family, and the mask-like expression on Mr X's face at certain

[1] 'Fallacies in Moral Philosophy', *Mind*, Vol. LVIII (1949), p. 476.

moments. G might be like the pop artist who reportedly commented on the play *Tiny Alice*, 'It was very boring, but then I do love to be bored.' Or G may feel that Mr X's life, despite some disagreeable features, is exquisitely stylized; and G's preference for stylization may lead him to oppose B's evaluation.

It is more than likely, however, that if B and G disagree in their evaluations they also will describe what they saw differently. It is likely, for example, that G will not describe as boring some of the activities which B describes as boring, or that G will not describe the family life he witnessed as 'superficial'. It is extremely likely that G, if he considers Mr X's life on the whole desirable, will not concur with B's claim to have witnessed the emptiness of Mr X's life.

It may be tempting to put a gloss on the difference in descriptions by saying 'G and B did see the same things, but they describe them differently.' But do G and B necessarily see the same things if they witness the same events? In order to answer this, we have to investigate the whole concept, in such cases, of 'seeing', and also have to investigate the variety of possible differences between B and G.

Let us suppose that B describes Mr X's relations with his family as 'superficial', and G describes them as 'stylized'. One possibility undoubtedly is that this difference in their summary descriptions is the only difference between B's and G's views of Mr X's relations with his family. In this case B and G will be willing to agree to a minute-by-minute narrative of X's behaviour towards his family. The only difference is that B sums up this behaviour as 'superficial', while G sums it up as 'stylized'.

It would be likely, however, that B and G would not be willing to agree to a minute-by-minute narrative of X's behaviour, and that on the level of detailed description there would be major differences between them. These differences may be of one or more of three kinds.

First, the description of particular actions may well differ. When Mr X speaks to his son, B may describe this as a vapid and rather cold dispensing of parental advice, while G may describe it as a dignified performance reminiscent of Lord Chesterfield. G may simply refuse to agree that B's manner was 'cold'. It would be typical in such cases for G not to offer a diametrically opposed description: very probably G will not describe Mr X's manner as 'warm', but simply will argue that the word 'cold' is not appropriate.

Secondly, some things may be given more stress in B's account than in G's, and vice versa. G may mention prominently Mr X's good manners, the lack of awkward pauses in his conversation, the general orderliness of the household. B may dwell on the fact that Mr X spent a long time talking on the telephone with business associates whom he admits he dislikes, or on the infrequency with which Mr X said that he shared activities with his children. There of course is an evaluative element involved in which episodes in a narrative assume importance. Presumably B stresses the things he does because he already places a highly negative value on elaborately polite and time-consuming relations with people one dislikes, and a positive value on close family relations. These values affect his view of Mr X's life, and may themselves be in part the result of earlier experience (or the authority of parents and teachers, or indirectly of the habits which they enforced). (To the extent that the values which influence B's view of Mr X may be in part the result of earlier experience, and to the extent that B's experience at Mr X's home may lead to value judgments which in turn will influence future experience, and to the extent also that B's judgments may be argued to be correct, we can appreciate Aristotle's remark that experience has given some men an eye with which they can see correctly. Someone who agrees with B's judgments can argue that earlier experiences of, say, the relations between parents and children may have given B an eye with which he can see the emptiness of Mr X's life.)

A third difference between B and G may be that some events are entirely left out of B's narrative which occur in G's narrative, or vice versa. It is possible that one of them simply noticed things which the other did not notice. Thus G may have noticed a placid smile on the face of Mr X's son at one point which B had not noticed. Or alternatively, B may have noticed a surly expression on the boy's face which G had not noticed. It is possible, also, that one of them attached significance to certain things, and saw connections, which the other did not. Thus both may have noticed the beautiful condition of the books in Mr X's library, but it occurred only to B that this indicated that probably the books were not very much used. Only G realized that Mr X's familiarity with baseball scores indicated that he probably did talk about sports with his son. Only B connected Mr X's frequent calls to a tax consultant with Mr X's repeated remark that in his opinion anything which was legal was also moral.

In connection with this kind of difference, it is worth reminding ourselves that some people are more 'perceptive' than others. (This too may be part of the meaning of Aristotle's remark that experience has given some men an eye with which they can see correctly. An experienced man may notice more, or see more connections, than one who lacks experience.) We may imagine B and G, after the weekend, viewing a motion picture of Mr X's activities during the weekend. B may get G to notice certain things that B had noticed. 'Notice the expression on his face at the moment when his wife leaves the room.' If B gets G to notice all of the things he noticed, and to make all of the connections which he made, this may end their disagreement. G may come to subscribe to B's account of Mr X's life, and to agree with his evaluation. However it is likely, because of the other possible grounds of disagreement which I have mentioned, that this would not happen. G and B may well notice the same things, make more or less the same connections, and still disagree.

At this point it should have emerged clearly that it is possible for G and B to witness the same events and yet not 'see' (in the sense of 'notice') the same things. But there is a further question. Let us suppose that G and B notice the same things, or, as we might say, that the same things 'register' on them. Does this entitle us to conclude unequivocally that they 'see' the same things? Or, if they give different descriptions, are we allowed the paradoxical conclusion that they 'see' the same things but yet 'see' something different?

It is impossible at this stage not to refer to the suggestive discussion of related problems in Wittgenstein's *Philosophical Investigations*. In Part II, xi, Wittgenstein discusses two uses of the word 'see'. In one, it makes sense to say that if B and G noticed the same things they saw the same thing. In the other, we may say of what we see that 'we interpret it, and *see* it as we *interpret* it'.[1] In this sense, if B and G produce sharply different narratives it appears that they 'saw' different things.

Here the whole concept of what 'experience' is comes into question. Wittgenstein suggests that when we see an object *as* something or other, we must first have mastered the concept of what we are seeing it as, which in turn involves mastering the technique of applying the concept. As Wittgenstein says,

[1] *Philosophical Investigations* (New York: Macmillan & Co., 1953), p. 193; italics are Wittgenstein's.

'But how queer for this to be the logical condition of someone's having such-and-such an *experience*! After all, you don't say that one only "has toothache" if one is capable of doing such-and-such. From this it follows that we cannot be dealing with the same concept of experience here. It is a different though related concept.'[1]

What Wittgenstein says is applicable clearly to B and G. B could not have had his experience at the home of Mr X unless he had mastered such concepts as those of 'an empty life' and 'superficial personal relations'. Such concepts are not used by everyone: they are not learned as part of traditional moral codes, and indeed it may be that our ethical traditions are to some extent deficient in teaching us the use of concepts related to style of life.[2] In at least this one respect B's experience is 'special' and 'learned'.

Something like this is true even with regard to concepts which are used more widely, and about whose use there are clearer standards. Take for example the concept of rudeness. Suppose a host tells a guest that he is an idiot, thus offending the man. Someone who knows about rudeness will experience this differently from someone, say a small child, who has not mastered the concept. Again, having mastered a concept is a pre-requisite for having a certain kind of experience.

It should be pointed out, of course, that if two people share a pre-requisite for an experience, this does not guarantee that when one has this experience the other will, even if they are witnessing the same events. G may have mastered the concept of an 'empty' life, at least well enough to convince us that he knows the meanings of the words, and yet not see Mr X's life as 'empty'. We may imagine T, U, and V all witnessing the rudeness of the host in our other example. They all, by ordinary standards, have mastered the concept of 'rudeness'. T sees the host's behaviour as 'crude and unforgivably rude'. U, who regards the host rather as Boswell regarded Dr Johnson, gives the concept of rudeness a twist, and sees the host as 'magnificently rude'. V considers the host's behaviour as justified, and sees his action as 'giving a justified reproof, and not really as rude'.

Now B can argue that G has not *really* mastered the concept of 'an empty life', and T can argue that U and V have not *really*

---

[1] *ibid.*, p. 208; italics are Wittgenstein's.
[2] Cf. my 'Confucius and the Problem of Naturalness', *Philosophy East and West*, July 1968.

mastered the concept of 'rudeness'; but what the matter really boils down to is that for a man to have an empty life, or even to be rude, is not quite like an apple being more than two inches in diameter.[1] It is no use trying to settle the question conclusively by appealing to the 'facts': as Hampshire points out,

'The word "fact," here as always is treacherous, involving the old confusion between the actual situation and the description of it; the situation is given, but not "the facts of the situation"; to state the facts is to analyse and interpret the situation.'[2]

The concepts that we use in ethics are not as precise as those used in grading apples or in physics. Their use is subject to difficulties in exceptional cases, and in general they are much more subject to arguments about their application. A group of people may have mastered the same ethical concepts, at least by ordinary, moderate standards, and yet may differ among themselves with regard to experiences and judgments.

When we confront differences in ethical experience, it may be tempting to analyse them as follows. We might abstract two components in an experience: one is the 'raw' experience, and the other is the interpretation which one infuses into the experience. Someone who does this might argue that T, U, and V have the same 'raw' experience (providing that the same events have 'registered' on them); and, with a similar provision, it might be argued also that B and G have the same 'raw' experience.

There are two difficulties with this. One is that the word 'interpretation' suggests the formulation of a hypothesis. But if V really *sees* the host's behaviour as 'not rude' he is not formulating a hypothesis: he rather is having a certain kind of experience. The same kind of thing can be said of B, G, T, and U. Thus it appears that to speak in such cases of 'interpreting', is to stretch considerably the meaning of 'interpret'.

Also there is something very questionable about the idea of 'raw' experience. It is hard to point to a case in which it occurs. Experiments with newborn infants have indicated that even they have ways of structuring experience which, say, newborn Martians might not share. It is true that there are experiences which one may have without having mastered a concept: such as having a toothache. But it appears also that a small child who has not

---

[1] Cf. J. O. Urmson, 'On Grading', *Mind*, Vol. LIX (1950).
[2] 'Fallacies in Moral Philosophy', *Mind*, Vol. LVIII (1949), fn. p. 476.

mastered the concept of toothache will have a different experience of toothache from that of an adult who has mastered the concept: the pain may not present itself as so clearly localized, for example. Thus even our simple experience of having a toothache hardly appears 'raw'. Nor will it do to say that, at least, the small child has a 'raw' experience of a toothache: it is quite conceivable that, had he been born on Mars, he would experience his toothache differently.

All of this suggests that any experience involves an element of something like 'seeing as'. We may, if we wish, attempt to abstract this element within an experience, and also may speak of a 'raw' element which we structure or organize in a certain way; but we must remember that this is as artificial as the distinction between content and form in literature, and that purely 'raw' experience appears to be as much an abstraction as formless content.

The aesthetic analogy suggests a further point. All literary works are in a style, but some works are much more stylized than others. In a similar manner it can be argued that, even if all experience involves an element of something like 'seeing as', this element is far more pronounced in some experiences than in others.

This element is clearly very pronounced in the experiences of B and G. It is perhaps less pronounced in the cases of T, U, V, and also A and D, and appears a good deal less pronounced in the case of C.

The case of C actually is an excellent example of one in which almost all observers would share, at least roughly, the same experiences. To the extent that there is an element of 'seeing as' in observing the effects of a theft upon its victim, it is one which almost all of us would share. It pertains to the common part of our moral backgrounds. It is no accident, of course, that the area in which we are most likely to have shared experience is also the one in which we are most likely to agree in our judgments. Almost everyone agrees that theft is wrong.

The case of A is complicated by the fact that what A experiences is so much affected by what he has experienced previously. Having worked with juvenile offenders amounts, in this case, to having a trained eye. Presumably those of us who do not have this eye will not see what A sees.

To the extent that A's training involves having mastered concepts, his will be a clear example of a case in which having mastered concepts is a pre-requisite for having certain experiences. In this respect, A's experiences may seem to involve as prominent an element of 'seeing as' as any experiences, including B's, could. Indeed it may appear that the cases of B and A really are parallel. B has mastered the concept of an 'empty life' etc. and thus sees the life of Mr X in a way in which not everyone would; A has mastered certain concepts in his work, and thus sees juvenile offenders in a way in which not everyone would.

There however are major differences between the two cases. One difference is this. A's manner of experiencing, and the ethical judgments which he makes as a result of experience, are intimately related, as I pointed out, to predictions. It is always logically possible to accept A's predictions of the behaviour of the juvenile offenders, and yet to dissent from his ethical evaluations; but the correctness of the predictions certainly creates a presumption in favour of, and gives authority to, the ethical evaluations. Similarly, if A's predictions are correct, this creates some presumption that the way in which he sees a juvenile offender is correct. Thus it is very easy to argue that there is 'objective' evidence which supports A's observations of the juvenile offenders.

This 'objective' evidence is not so essentially and closely relevant in the case of B. It is true that B's experience also may be related to predictions: B may correctly predict Mr X's suicide, or more prosaically that Mr X will get ulcers. But it seems easier for us to acknowledge B's skill in predicting while rejecting both his general view of Mr X's life and his ethical judgment of that life than it is to acknowledge A's skill in predicting while rejecting both his view and his evaluation of the juvenile offender. It would not be difficult to feel that B has grasped some tendencies of Mr X's life, but has seen them through a jaundiced eye, or has mistakenly viewed tragic elements as base and contemptible.

Indeed B's experience and judgment of Mr X can stand independently of predictions in a way in which A's experience and judgment of the juvenile offender cannot. It would be strange if A said 'He is not so bad', and then refused to make predictions. It would not sound strange for B to term Mr X's life 'empty', and then to admit that he had little idea of what Mr X's life would be like in the future.

A second major difference between the cases of A and B appears to be as follows. Suppose that everyone in America is exposed to uses of the concepts on which A and B rely, and is exposed to the events to which they previously have been exposed. (I am formulating it this way in order to sidestep the troublesome, but not crucial, issue of what counts as real 'mastery' of concepts like that of an 'empty life'.) If everyone in America then were confronted with the behaviour of the juvenile offender and with the events of the weekend at Mr X's, it seems likely that a much greater number of people would share A's experience of the juvenile offender in important respects than would share B's experience of the weekend at Mr X's.

If this is correct it would help to account for the feeling (which I think would constitute almost everyone's first reaction) that B's experiences (and ethical judgment) are more 'personal', and perhaps more 'subjective', than A's. It is worth pointing out, though, that even if it is true that most Americans can be brought to share A's experiences more readily than B's experiences, this arguably does not express any intrinsic difference between the characters of the experiences, but rather illumines a fact about our culture. One way of putting this is to say that B's experiences require an 'outlook' which is not entirely common in our culture; this is not (or at least need not be) true of A's experiences. Outside of our culture, the status of the two experiences might be quite different. A's experiences might appear quite 'personal' and 'subjective' to the inhabitants of a Zen monastery, whereas to the Zen monks the emptiness of 'meaninglessness' of someone's life might appear as visible and 'objective' as sadness or aggressiveness appear to us.

The case of D may be like that of A, if D is a trained psychologist or a man of deep and unusual experience, and may be like that of B if D's experiences reflect an uncommon general outlook. In the respects in which it can be varied, D's case is like a great many cases of people arriving at ethical judgments as a result of experience. Experience always can be affected by the possession of a trained eye, or by previous experience; experience always may, also, reflect either a common or an uncommon general outlook.

What I have tried to show thus far is not the existence of a simple common element in cases like those of A, B, C, and D, but rather the existence and possibility of variations. Each of the 'stories' which these cases represent could of course be varied considerably. Thus it appears that the safest generalizations about experience in ethics will take the form 'Experience *may* have such-and-such characteristics, and such-and-such a role', rather than the form 'Experience *must* have such-and-such characteristics, and such-and-such a role'.

III

This suggests two points. One is that it is especially important, in discussing problems such as we have been discussing, to have a variety of examples. Relying on one kind of case can lead to a one-sided or over-simple picture.

One reason why it is important to mention this is that the error has been committed. Many contemporary philosophers have been extremely preoccupied with the role of rules and principles in ethics, and have concentrated on the generalizations which we invoke in debate and justification of our ethical judgments. This has been accompanied by a preoccupation with judgments that certain things are in general morally wrong or morally obligatory: e.g. judgments that murder is wrong, that one is morally obliged to help defenceless poor people, that it is wrong to imprison debtors.

Of the four cases at the beginning of this chapter only C's involves an ethical judgment which clearly implies or is implied by a judgment that certain things are in general morally wrong or morally obligatory. It might be argued that D's judgment implies a general judgment that people in a position very similar to his ought to make a similar decision; but even if this is so D may contend that the implicit general judgment is not moral, since he would not say of someone who chose differently in very similar circumstances that his choice was *morally* wrong. B's judgment also is clearly an ethical judgment, but perhaps not a moral judgment: after all, B can condemn Mr X's life as empty without claiming that anything that he does is morally wrong.[1] A's judg-

---

[1] A word should be said about the terms 'moral' and 'ethical'. These terms are used in a variety of ways by various philosophers, and some philosophers use them almost interchangeably. I am endeavouring, however, to follow one strand of ordinary usage with respect to them. In ordinary usage, there is no moral problem which would not also be called an ethical problem; but there are problems which sometimes are called ethical problems but which we hesitate to call moral problems. The problem of whether to commit a murder or not would commonly be called either a moral or an ethical problem. If a man wonders whether it is best to devote his leisure time to intellectual and aesthetic pursuits, or whether he should forget intellectual matters and spend his time bowling, most people would be willing to call this an ethical problem: after all, it is the kind of problem Plato, Aristotle, John Stuart Mill, and Moore all were keenly concerned with in their work in ethics. But very few people would call this a moral problem.

To examine in detail the complicated grounds of distinction between what would commonly be called either an ethical or a moral judgment, and what might be called an ethical but not a moral judgment, would involve an excessively long digression from the main line of argument. Two factors which are related to the

ment is a particular judgment of character; and, while it is a moral judgment, the only general judgment which it implies is that people who are of a certain kind are 'not so bad'.

The case of C is the one of our four in which experience pretty clearly did not increase one's right to be confident of the ethical judgment. It also is the one of the four which seemed least markedly tinctured by elements of 'seeing as'. Thus it is understandable that a philosopher who was preoccupied with general judgments of what is morally obligatory or morally wrong might overlook the important role of experience in ethics, and also, if he discussed experience at all, might overlook the element of something like 'seeing as' which so often is prominent in ethical experience.

It may be argued that all of this is related to a serious blindness on the part of many philosophers to the most pressing ethical issues of our time. Consider for example the judgment, in some ways reminiscent of B's, that a person growing up in a society which is heavily 'concerned with production or with the sale and consumption of things' becomes

'more and more like a thing himself. . . . And under these circumstances any person must begin to feel lonely and anxious, because it becomes increasingly difficult to see the real meaning of life beyond simply that of making a living; (thus he) becomes bored and then undertakes to overcome it by more and more change in consumption and by the seeking of thrills in what may well be meaningless excitement. And his thinking or his being then becomes split from emotions, and his truth from any kind of commitment, and I suppose his mind also from his heart.'[1]

---

distinction may, however, be noted. One is this. To rest on traditionally accepted broad principles (e.g. 'Murder is wrong', 'Adultery is wrong'), or on broad principles which may be proposed to stand alongside these traditional principles (e.g. 'It is wrong to imprison debtors', 'One should give substantial assistance to the poor') clearly is conducive to classification as 'moral'. A second factor involves the way in which moral disapproval invites the community to apply pressure against an offender to an especially high degree. This implies restraint on our part in treating judgments as moral. Thus if behaviour lies in an area which we are inclined to consider a man's 'own business' (e.g. whether he prefers the contemplative life or bowling), we are that much less likely to consider our judgments of it to be moral judgments.

For a distinction similar to mine, see P. F. Strawson 'Social Morality and Individual Ideals', *Philosophy* Vol. XXXVI (1961).

[1] Eugene McCarthy, in a speech to the Fellowship of Reconciliation, quoted in *The New York Review*, July 11, 1968, p. 6.

McCarthy of course is not saying that the behaviour of the people he describes is morally wrong, and the claim that he is making pretty clearly is an ethical claim but not a moral claim. Whether he is right or not, his claim is a good deal more important than are many general judgments of moral obligation or wrongness. Yet claims of this kind have not been much discussed in recent philosophical literature.

McCarthy's claim, like B's, suggests a basis in experience. It would be impossible to discuss the claim adequately without discussing the observations which might lead to it. This suggests that closer attention to the variety of roles which experience plays in ethics would go hand in hand with better appreciation of the variety of ethical problems.

A second point is this. One philosopher whose conception of experience, and of its possible role in ethics, ought by now to have emerged as especially simple is A. J. Ayer.

Let us re-examine some of Ayer's claims in the light of what we have been discussing. Ayer claims that 'actual ethical judgments' are not logical claims, cannot be empirically verified, and hence lack literal meaning. He divides statements which are empirically verifiable into two classes: statements which are directly verifiable, and statements which are indirectly verifiable. A statement is 'directly verifiable if it is either itself an observation-statement, or is such that in conjunction with one or more observation-statements it entails at least one observation-statement which is not deducible from these other premises alone . . .'.[1] A statement is 'indirectly verifiable if it satisfies the following conditions: first, that in conjunction with certain other premises it entails one or more directly verifiable statements which are not deducible from these other premises alone; and secondly, that these other premises do not include any statement that is not either analytic, or directly verifiable, or capable of being independently established as indirectly verifiable'.[2]

It seems to me that there is a good case to be made for saying that both B's statement and Senator McCarthy's statement meet Ayer's conditions for direct verifiability. For clearly both may be, in some sense, making 'observation-statements': they are reporting what they have observed. Ayer defines 'observation-statement' to mean a statement 'which records an actual or possible observation'.[3] This

---

[1] *Language Truth and Logic* (New York: Dover Books, 1947), p. 13.
[2] *loc. cit.*   [3] *ibid.*, p. 11.

certainly seems to fit these two cases, with the qualification that Senator McCarthy's statement might be argued to record a large collection of observations rather than a single observation.

I suspect that Ayer would have two difficulties in agreeing to this. One is a difficulty which I developed in Chapter IV. B's statement and Senator McCarthy's statement would be unlikely to attract the kind of consensus which we expect to surround scientific claims; the problems which they attack are unlikely to be 'settled' in the way in which scientific problems often appear to be settled. Ayer's remarks indicate that there is an implicit appeal to consensus in his use of the word 'verification'. Thus he probably would argue, for example, that B's 'observation' does not constitute 'verification' of B's claim (and that if another person saw what B saw this too would not count as 'verification'). This would lead him, I suspect, to deny that B's statement indeed does count as an 'observation statement'.

But what if we are all converted, we all see what B sees, and we all regard this as establishing B's claim? In the world which then would exist, it would be more difficult for Ayer to deny that what B says is an 'observation statement', or that B's claim is 'verified'. This suggests, as I argued in Chapter IV, that a good deal of the plausibility of Ayer's view depends on the entirely contingent truth that there happens to be a good deal of ethical disagreement in our world.

Ayer might also object that B's statement is not an 'observation statement', in the way in which 'The dial points to 5.3' is an observation statement, because B's statement is so 'interpretative', or involves such a prominent element of something like 'seeing as'. Here it is worth recalling the argument that any experience involves an element of something like 'seeing as'. Certainly a laboratory assistant cannot have the experience of seeing a dial pointing to 5.3 unless he has mastered relevant concepts.

B's experience may seem much more 'interpretative' than that of the laboratory assistant, but why? One factor may be that the concepts B has to master are more complex, and less precise: the rules for their application are not firmly established. However it is worth recalling what Wittgenstein points out about rules in *Philosophical Investigations*. The rules for the use of the concepts upon which the laboratory assistant relies are never finally and completely spelled out. They cannot be. The establishment of rules depends, ultimately, on an agreement in forms of behaviour. This agreement *could* exist with regard to B's concepts within a community (say one like a Zen monastery): it again is a contingent truth that it does not exist within mid-twentieth century America.

This brings us back to the fact of ethical diversity. Now this diversity is greater on some matters than on others, and we can imagine a continuum with regard to this of observations and ethical judgments which B might make. Suppose that B sees Mr Y beat his wife and children, with no provocation, and B says that he has observed Mr Y's brutality. There probably are some people who feel that random violence, within certain broad limits, is an important prerogative of the head of a household. These people presumably would see Mr Y's behaviour differently, and would deny that he really was 'brutal'. But people like this are rare; and it seems likely that almost all civilized people would see, and judge, Mr Y's behaviour much as B does.

Suppose that B sees the host calling his guest an idiot, and says that he has seen the host behaving rudely. Suppose also that B sees a man spending on his own amusements some of the money which his wife and children badly need. B says that he has seen the man behaving irresponsibly.

Do we assert that none of B's statements may be an observation statement? 'Mr Y was brutal' appears to be able to attract about as much consensus as many statements made in the laboratory, and in many cases the word 'brutal' can function as part of what we might want to label an 'objective' description of what one has seen. ('What did you see?' 'I saw some brutal behaviour'.) Mrs Philippa Foot has made somewhat related claims about the word 'rude'.[1]

If we do assert that none of B's statements is an observation statement, we seem to be left with a very narrow conception of an 'observation'. A genuine observation then appears to be one which any person devoid of ethical concepts is capable of, providing only that he has been taught the appropriate scientific concepts. On the other hand, if we wish to assert that some of B's statements are observation statements, and that others are not, it is very difficult to draw a line among them. It is hard to admit 'He behaved brutally' as an observation statement, and yet to deny that 'He was rude' can be an observation statement. It is hard to admit 'He was

---

[1] 'Moral Arguments', *Mind*, Vol. LXVII (1958). My previous remarks however should indicate that I believe that there is normally more room for argument about whether some behaviour is rude than Mrs Foot appears to allow.

rude' as an observation statement, and yet to deny that 'He has behaved irresponsibly' can be an observation statement. It is hard to admit 'He has behaved irresponsibly' as an observation statement, and yet to deny that 'His life is empty' can be an observation statement.

There are problems also surrounding the status of the statements made by A, C, and D. These statements appear to be logically related to actual or possible observation, although the logical relations arguably are not as simple as those Ayer stipulates. Let us suppose that A assumes the principle, 'Boys who are not so bad will not repeat their offences (except under extremely mitigating circumstances).' The conjunction of this principle with A's judgment that the juvenile offender is 'not so bad' entails a set of observation statements about the boy's future behaviour in various sets of circumstances. The principle which supplies the added premise is not analytic: there is no flat contradiction in saying that a boy is not so bad, but will continue to steal hubcaps. The principle also is not directly verifiable, or indirectly verifiable in some independent way. Thus A's judgment does not quite meet Ayer's conditions for 'indirect verifiability'. But it is worth pointing out again that it is given logical support by observations of the boy's future behaviour: the case for regarding A as having been right is greatly strengthened if the boy does not commit any further offences. The logical support which observations may give to A's judgment, in other words, is not quite what Ayer specifies; but it is real enough.

Something similar may be said about the judgments made by C and D. Let us suppose that both assume the principle that 'It is better that an action not be performed if it leads to greater unhappiness than happiness'. This principle itself is not verifiable, and arguably it is not analytic. (Kant, whatever his faults, does not advocate a self-contradictory view.) Together with the judgment that C should not have stolen from the shopkeeper, the principle entails observation statements concerning the unhappiness produced by C's action. Together with the judgment that D should not remain with his mother, it entails observation statements concerning the unhappiness which would be produced if D remains with his mother. Again, C's observations or the observations which we might make of the general unhappiness if D remains at home, give logical support to their judgments: the case for accepting these judgments is stronger than it would be if we observed general ecstasy on the part of everyone who is stolen from, or if we observed thorough happiness on everyone's part if D remained at home.

Enough has been said to indicate clearly the narrowness and artificiality of the criteria which Ayer uses to deny literal meaning to ethical claims. It may be said, of course, that any philosopher can invent criteria to suit himself, and can use technical terms like 'literal meaning' in any way he chooses. In *Language Truth and Logic*, it might be said, Ayer simply played his own game by his own rules. There is another side to the picture, however: not only what Ayer said, but what Ayer left out. Ayer, and philosophers sympathetic to his view, did not do justice to the variety of roles which experience does play in ethical judgment. He did not indicate any way of dealing adequately with cases like those of A, B, C, and D. To say that experience does not have quite the same role in ethics that it has in the sciences is to give a very small part of the story.

CHAPTER VII
REASON IN ETHICS

There are two major inducements for discussing at this point the role of reason in ethics. One is that any positive account of the role of reason in ethics will contribute to my argument that there is ethical knowledge, since after all we tend to consider subjects 'cognitive' in which reason plays a part. The other inducement is that it is important that the argument that there is ethical knowledge rest on solid foundations. Some recent writers have formulated a 'cognitivist' position in such a way as to create an impression that the role of reason in ethics is more major and more conclusive than in my opinion it is. The firmness of my own case will be increased if I indicate the differences of my view from theirs, thus indicating the respects in which my view is more defensible.

My discussion will concentrate on two works: Stephen Toulmin's *An Examination of the Place of Reason in Ethics*, and Kurt Baier's *The Moral Point of View*. In each case I shall indicate what I am inclined to agree with in the work, and shall question what seems to me most questionable.

I

A fundamental question which Toulmin asks about reason in ethics is 'Which of the reasons (which we offer in support of ethical conclusions) are good reasons?'[1] The fact that Toulmin is willing to consider this question legitimate, and ultimately to answer it, immediately distinguishes him from philosophers such as Stevenson. One may recall Stevenson's remark that 'The reasons which support or attack an ethical judgment . . . subject to some exceptions . . . are related to the judgment psychologically rather than logically.'[2] Toulmin is searching for logical connections, of which Stevenson denies the existence.

It is clear that on this very basic point Toulmin is right. There are good reasons, and also poor reasons, in ethics. 'It makes people insecure and apprehensive about their possessions, and discourages hard work' is a good reason for saying that stealing is wrong. 'It

---

[1] Cf. *The Place of Reason in Ethics* (Cambridge: Cambridge University Press, 1961), p. 3.

[2] *Ethics and Language* (New Haven: Yale University Press, 1960), p. 113.

uses energy that could be devoted to sports' is a rather poor reason. Plainly there is considerable interest in determining which kinds of reasons in ethics are good and which kinds are poor. This is one of Toulmin's tasks. Instead of working with a variety of examples, however, and driving conclusions from his examination of these, Toulmin takes a short-cut. He approaches the question of the goodness of reasons by means of a principle. The principle relates logic to function. 'Can we discover', he asks, 'from our knowledge of the kinds of human situation and activity in which ethical sentences find their primary use, the kinds of thing that are relevant as arguments for one course of action or another?'[1] By analysing the function of ethics, Toulmin expects to find the key factor which determines the goodness of reasons.

The assumption underlying this short-cut is open to challenge, and indeed a strong case has been made against it by George Kerner.[2] However, since Kerner has not entirely convinced me, I shall initiate my criticism of Toulmin at another point. Let us assume for the sake of argument that Toulmin is justified in taking his short-cut: that the function of ethics does indeed provide the key to what determines the goodness of reasons. Let us examine what, according to Toulmin, is the function of ethics.

Toulmin suggests that this is 'to correlate our feelings and behaviour in such a way as to make the fulfilment of everyone's aims and desires as far as possible compatible'.[3] He appears to believe that ethics does this by erecting moral codes: that a moral code within a society, if it does the job that it is intended to do, correlates feelings and behaviour in such a way as to make the fulfilment of everyone's aims and desires as far as possible compatible.

This suggests the existence of two kinds of good reasons in ethics. There are good reasons which locate something as approved of or disapproved of by the code of one's society, and there also are good reasons which go beyond the code to the ultimate function of moral codes, and which show that what is being considered will cause or 'avoid causing to other members of the community some inconvenience, annoyance, or suffering. . .'.[4]

One of the most attractive features of Toulmin's book is his acknowledgment of what he is leaving out. He is willing to mention

[1] The Place of Reason in Ethics, p. 84.
[2] The Revolution in Ethical Theory (Oxford: Oxford University Press, 1966), pp. 112–16.
[3] The Place of Reason in Ethics, p. 137.   [4] ibid., p. 132.

the fact that 'compatibility of aims and desires' could be achieved 'on various levels of excellence'.[1] He is willing also to acknowledge that people reason in relation to the 'personal' decision of which things 'we expect to bring deeper and more lasting contentment'.[2] With regard to this reasoning Toulmin remarks that 'Perhaps the chief value of discovering how much of the logic of ethics can be formalized lies in seeing why so much of it cannot . . .', a remark with which I heartily concur.[3]

These acknowledgments do great credit to Toulmin's humanistic sensibility. Nevertheless he regards all of this as being on the fringes of his subject. Perhaps people ought to have good aesthetic taste, and ought to seek to lead contemplative lives; but 'One would never think of using examples of this kind when teaching anyone the notion of what he "ought" or "ought not" to do . . .'.[4]

There is an obvious degree of truth in this. But it is worth pointing out that it suggests a view in which the problems on which Books I and X of the *Nichomachean Ethics*, and also the last chapter of *Principia Ethica*, concentrate are regarded as far from the central matter of ethics. Perhaps this is because these problems are not what Toulmin would call 'moral' problems.[5] Toulmin appears to use the word 'moral' to cover ground similar to that which it covers in the use I set forth towards the end of the last chapter. In my use part of ethics consists of morals, and part of ethics (including what is dealt with in Books I and X of the *Nichomachean Ethics*, and the last chapter of *Principia Ethica*) does not. This suggests that Toulmin should have entitled his book *The Place of Reason in Morals*.

It is at least somewhat plausible to say that the function of morality is 'to correlate our feelings and behaviour in such a way as to make the fulfilment of everyone's aims and desires as far as possible compatible'. It is highly implausible to claim that this is *the* function of ethics, since so much of the best ethical thinking has been devoted to asking what way of life a man, *given* a place in a viable moral community, should find most desirable. If morality enables us to 'avoid causing to other members of the community . . . inconvenience, annoyance, or suffering . . .', what the remainder of ethics offers is, or ought to be, something more positive.

It might be tempting to admit all of this, but then to maintain that after all morality is the 'essential' part of ethics, and that moral considerations always outweigh other kinds of ethical considerations.

---

[1] *ibid.*, fn. p. 137. [2] *ibid.*, p. 157. [3] *ibid.*, p. 158. [4] *ibid.*, fn. p. 137.
[5] Cf. *loc. cit.*, also pp. 157–8.

In a sense this may come close to being trivially true, since when any consideration comes to seem very urgent to many people (and thus prompts us to that readiness for community pressure which is characteristic of morality), we become inclined to call it a moral consideration. We do not have a moral obligation to listen to good music, or to play records of good music for our friends; but if all of the scores and recordings of Mozart's music were about to be destroyed we would have a moral obligation to preserve them (for the benefit, it might be said, of posterity).[1] So that it could be argued that moral considerations always outweigh non-moral considerations. However, some of my examples in the previous chapter (those of the weekend at Mr X's, and of the alleged effects of living in a producing-consuming society) suggest a contrary view. There appear to be cases in which what should be very weighty considerations are apparent to relatively few people, and are considered even by those who take them seriously to be part of a man's own business: these 'arguably' weighty considerations are not termed 'moral'.

In any event the real question is 'Do considerations of inconvenience, annoyance, or suffering always outweigh other considerations?' The answer pretty clearly is 'No'. We can see this if we imagine a choice between having, on one hand, a society in which inconvenience, annoyance, or suffering were minimized, but in which the arts and all human relations were vapid and uninteresting, and, on the other hand, a society in which there was only slightly more inconvenience, annoyance, or suffering, but in which the arts and human relations displayed a good deal more flair, enthusiasm, and subtlety. It would require an extraordinary preoccupation with pain and suffering to prefer the former. Most of us, if we reflect even a little, can see that there are many things which we value quite as much as the absence of inconvenience, annoyance, or suffering: concentrated intellectual activity, aesthetic experiences of some subtlety and interest, warmth in personal relations, etc. If these factors conflict with the absence of inconvenience, annoyance, or suffering, we may well judge that the absence of inconvenience, annoyance, or suffering is not a decisive reason for saying that we ought to do something.

[1] We might not feel the same obligation to preserve recordings of Lawrence Welk, even if as many people like (and will like) them. Presumably the intrinsic value of the aesthetic experiences is a crucial factor. This appears to be a counter-example to Jan Narveson's denials that '. . . statements about intrinsic value per se may be admitted among the premises of moral arguments'. Cf. *Morality and Utility* (Baltimore: Johns Hopkins Press, 1967), p. 70.

Imagine the following dialogue.

A. You ought to vote for the XYZ proposal: your vote may well be decisive.
B. What will the proposal accomplish?
A. It will enable the government to impose and maintain minimum standards of comfort, even for hippies and derelicts who claim that they do not want to be comfortable.
B. What will the long-range effects of this be?
A. It will promote the existence of a society like that in Huxley's *Brave New World*.
B. What are the advantages of this society?
A. It will involve the minimum of inconvenience, annoyance, or suffering.
B. No thank you.

In this case not only is 'It involves the minimum of inconvenience, annoyance, or suffering' not a decisive reason, it arguably is not even a *good* reason. It is worth emphasizing that the question would generally be regarded as a moral question. A may well feel that B is morally obligated to vote for the XYZ proposal, in order to bring about the relief of so much suffering. Most of us, on the other hand, would feel that a society like *Brave New World* would be so horrendous that one is morally obligated to prevent it from coming into being.

It may be that in fact this is not a counter-example against anything that Toulmin says. Toulmin distinguishes in some places between arguments to justify a practice, and arguments which relate an individual case to a practice. Appeals to what would cause the minimum of inconvenience, annoyance, and suffering would have a place only within arguments of the former kind. The argument between A and B about voting for the XYZ proposal may be said not to be an argument about a practice (although something closely related to the institution of a moral practice is at stake). Clearly what A and B are discussing is not what we ordinarily would call a 'test case'. It might be argued that established principles, concerning freedom etc., would be decisive in the argument between A and B; and that, even in Toulmin's view, considerations of inconvenience, annoyance, and suffering would not enter into the question.

In view of this, it is worth presenting another version of the example. Suppose that the XYZ proposal has been passed some time ago, and has become part of not only the law but also the moral fabric of our community. The efficacy of the XYZ proposal depends on citizen co-operation, and almost everyone feels obligated to do his part in making it work. Specifically, almost everyone feels obligated to report himself to government comfort agents when he is (over a period of time) uncomfortable or suffering, and almost everyone feels obligated to report any other person who is clearly uncomfortable or suffering. A dialogue might proceed as follows:

A. Your uncle has been struggling for some time to write that symphony: his aspirations have made him extremely tense and unhappy.
B. It is true that he is restless and dissatisfied with himself, but he keeps saying 'Better Beethoven dissatisfied than a satisfied pig'.
A. You know you ought to report him to the government comfort agents.
B. Why?
A. Reporting him fulfils 'a "duty" to the "moral code" of the community' to which we belong.[1]
B. That does not seem convincing to me. Is this moral code really justified? Perhaps we ought to change it?
A. But the practice of reporting uncomfortable people to the government comfort agents helps to prevent suffering among members of the community.

A may in addition argue that dissatisfaction is contagious, so that B, by reporting his uncle, not only will prevent his further suffering, but also will prevent still other people from suffering.

Again, not only is 'It involves a minimum of inconvenience, annoyance, or suffering' not a decisive reason, it arguably is not even a good reason. It should be clear, moreover, that this version of the example is one in which both types of consideration which Toulmin mentions on page 132 are relevant to, and support, a course of action which most of us would nevertheless argue to be mistaken.

The most obvious comment is this. If we are going to appeal to consequences in evaluating a practice, 'inconvenience, annoyance, or suffering' is too narrow a selection: there may well be more important elements within the consequences of a practice. Toulmin himself appears aware of this. At one point, after remarking that

[1] *The Place of Reason in Ethics*, p. 132.

'often enough moral considerations do not take us all the way', he says that in criticizing institutions we can inquire whether, '. . . if some specific change were made, the members of our community would lead fuller and happier lives'.[1] Elsewhere, in discussing judgment of a moral practice, or judgment of a case with regard to which current principles conflict, Toulmin speaks simply of estimating 'the probable consequences'.[2]

My impression is that Toulmin never fully made up his mind as to the relation between morality and the fringe areas of ethics whose existence he acknowledges. Consequently he never fully made up his mind as to the respects in which consequences other than those involving 'inconvenience, annoyance, and suffering' were relevant to arguments about a moral practice. The important point though is this. It is somewhat easier to gain agreement concerning the inconvenience, annoyance, and suffering which a moral practice produces, than it is to gain agreement concerning whether the lives it produces are 'fuller and happier'. It is extremely difficult to gain consensus concerning the height of the 'level of excellence' at which compatibility of aims and desires is achieved.

What I am getting at may be put this way. If we judge moral practices by their consequences, and judge them narrowly (taking into account only inconvenience, annoyance, and suffering) then our test may seem fairly 'objective': almost everyone may arrive at roughly the same judgment. This will especially be the case at some time in the future if the social sciences provide a highly developed and precise manner of estimating the consequences of moral practices and their alternatives, and if the social sciences also provide fairly precise ways of measuring what we normally call 'suffering', etc.

If, however, we judge moral practices by their consequences in this narrow way, our answers often will be quite questionable. In the case over which A and B argued, most of us would consider the answer given by a narrow appeal to consequences to be wrong. Thus this test, while it may be fairly 'objective', does not seem reliable.

If we judge moral practices by their consequences in a broad manner, on the other hand, the test will seem far less 'objective'. No one expects that the social sciences will ever be able to tell us whether Aristotle's view of what 'happiness' really is, is correct. No one expects the social sciences to provide fairly precise tests of

[1] *The Place of Reason in Ethics*, p. 159.   [2] *ibid.*, pp. 147, 150.

levels of excellence of community life to which almost everyone can agree.

Now none of these remarks should be interpreted as expressing scepticism about the usefulness of reasons in ethics, or as suggesting that Stevenson was right after all. Rather they suggest a more qualified view of the role of reasons in ethics than Toulmin presents. We can develop this view after we examine the claims about the role of reason in ethics contained in Kurt Baier's *The Moral Point of View*.

II

Baier is much more explicitly concerned than Toulmin to develop a 'cognitivist' position, and much more explicitly concerned also to stress the role of reason as a heuristic tool in enabling us to arrive at moral judgments. The 'cognitivism' is stated quite early. He lists, as one of the 'four main logical features of moral judgments', 'that we often know whether a course of action is right or wrong even though obviously we cannot perceive it by means of one of our senses'.[1] There is moral knowledge, but we cannot account for moral knowledge by means of our five senses, or of a moral sense. The alternative explanation is in terms of reason.

Thus Baier claims flatly that 'judgments to the effect that a certain course of action is morally right or morally wrong express "natural", if complicated facts. They state that the course of action in question has the weight of moral reasons behind or against it'.[2] ' "The best thing to do" means "the course supported by the best reason".'[3]

What are we to make of these claims? At the core there is something which verges on the unexceptionable. It is not easy to disagree with the claim that the best course of action in a situation always will be supported by the best reasons, or the reasons with the most weight. Certainly it is very difficult to produce a case in which a course of action which is not the best has the strongest collection of reasons supporting it. One may well ask 'How could a wrong, or inferior, course of action in the last analysis have the strongest reasons behind it?'

Embedded in this, is the truth that some reasons used in moral argument are stronger or 'better' than others, and that some collections of reasons have more weight than others. If a man is consider-

---

[1] *The Moral Point of View* (Ithaca: Cornell University Press, 1958), p. v.
[2] *ibid.*, p. vi.   [3] *ibid.*, p. 87.

ing abandoning his benefactor on a desert island, 'You should not harm someone who has helped you' would be a good reason against the deed, as would 'There is no food supply on the island, so that would be murder!' 'This will enable me to have money to buy books' is an inferior reason in support of the action, and clearly would be far outweighed by the reasons against it.

It is possible to imagine cases in which something is right even though there are strong reasons against it. If, in an unfairly managed and uncharitable society, a man is justified in stealing in order to buy medicine for his desperately ill children, almost all of the familiar reasons against theft would weigh against his action. But it would appear that, if we agree that his theft would be justified, we agree also that his children's needs provide a reason of weight at least equal to the others. Thus it would appear that, in any case which represents an exception to a familiar rule, some mitigating reason of adequate strength will be found, even if it is only one of those accessible even to very inarticulate people e.g. 'The consequences will be disastrous'.

It may seem, on the basis of what I have said thus far, that I stand ready to concede to Baier all that he needs. Certainly I am ready to concede the extreme plausibility of a good deal of what Baier says, at least in the abstract. However there are three points, two of which in my judgment are extremely important, at which I am inclined to be doubtful.

The first point is this: it is not entirely clear that 'the best thing to do' *means* 'the course supported by the best reasons'. That there is room for doubt can be seen as follows. Let us suppose that a philosopher claims, along lines reminiscent of Kierkegaard, that A is a better thing to do than B, even though B is supported by better reasons. The claim that the best thing to do sometimes is not the alternative supported by the best reasons, may be false in the moral sphere; but, even if it is, it is hard to argue that it involves a demonstrable contradiction. We certainly can understand the claim of someone who says 'It is best for Abraham to be prepared to kill Isaac, even though it is not supported by the best reasons', in a way in which we would not understand the claim of someone who said 'The best reasons support Abraham's being prepared to kill Isaac, but they do not support it'. This suggests that 'the best thing to do' does not mean 'the course supported by the best reasons'.

The second point is one to which I attach a great deal more importance. It seems to me that Baier, when he identifies rightness with support by the strongest reasons, conflates the facts of a situation and the reasons applicable to a decision regarding it. I wish to suggest that there is an important gap between, on one hand, what is the case *vis-à-vis* a moral problem, and on the other hand what we can say about the moral problem, of which Baier does not adequately take note.

Let me illustrate the difficulties here by means of a concrete example. We can develop the example in considerable detail, and see how well what Baier says applies to it.

Let us suppose that Brutus is deliberating over whether to kill Caesar. A number of considerations clearly are relevant, both supporting and opposing a decision to kill Caesar. On one hand, to kill Caesar would be murder, and thus *prima facie* wrong. There also are all of the arguments against killing Caesar which generally may be used against murder. To kill a man deprives him of the pleasure of living. It may well cause anguish to his family and friends. It may well produce a guilty conscience in the man who commits the murder (or, conversely, increase his tendency towards violence), and thus (in one way or another) poison his psychological life. Murder also has an effect on society. It increases insecurity and suspicion on the part of anyone who thinks that there is any chance of his being murdered. It also encourages similar acts, by a kind of moral contagion. The possibility of murder may seem more vivid to angry or violent men if Brutus murders Caesar. In addition, it is possible that Brutus' outstanding reputation may make murder seem slightly more 'respectable' if he murders Caesar, thus perhaps encouraging some people to commit murders who otherwise would be ashamed. Besides this, there is the fact of a special relation between Brutus and Caesar. Caesar has been kind to Brutus, and it is *prima facie* wrong to injure a benefactor. Such an act, again, discourages kindness and promotes insecurity and suspicion.

On the other hand, it is arguable that Caesar, by his totalitarian tendencies, has forfeited his right to gratitude or protection. It is arguable also that a free society is in great danger of losing its freedom, that Caesar systematically is subverting the republican institutions of Rome. It is arguable further that the good effects of killing Caesar, which may include the recovery of these institutions, would be of such magnitude as to outweigh the bad effects of killing Caesar. Furthermore, if Brutus kills Caesar, this may provide such a notable example of public-spirited taking of risks that it may encourage brave and public-spirited actions throughout the Roman world.

Three things about this problem must be pointed out immediately. First, it is a moral problem. It is a moral problem even if Brutus, when he makes his decision, claims that the situation is so unique and difficult that his decision does not embody any principle general enough to be applied to any case which is not virtually indentical with the one with which Brutus is confronted. I should think that we would all tend to call Brutus' problem a moral problem simply because it involves murder, and we have a strong general tendency to call problems involving murder moral problems. I should think, also, that we all would tend to say that Brutus approached his problem *as* a moral problem if he weighed, and gave serious attention to, some of the considerations I have mentioned, even if in the last analysis he claims that he cannot articulate what he regarded as decisive in the form of a principle of more than minimal generality. I shall say more about this shortly.

Secondly, Brutus' problem is a difficult problem. I myself am inclined to believe, on the basis of very incomplete knowledge of the circumstances, that Brutus (judging on the basis of what he was in a position to know) should have decided not to kill Caesar. Certainly the results of his action suggest that he made the wrong choice. However, it is worth pointing out, just so that we can take Brutus' problem seriously, that there clearly are some cases in which it would be right to kill a dictator. Most of us would agree, for example, that someone should have killed Hitler. Almost everyone would agree that if a mad dictator is about to take steps which would lead very directly to blowing up the world, he should be killed. Thus, even if Brutus (as I think) did not make the most wise decision, we cannot treat the solution to his problem as glaringly obvious.

Thirdly, it is important to realize how difficult—perhaps impossible—it is to spell out in adequate detail the factors relevant to Brutus' choice. Take for example the considerations which I said would weigh against Brutus' killing Caesar. One is the anguish which the deed would cause to Caesar's family and friends. In normal cases, murder is so clearly wrong that there is no need to examine this factor in any detail. But here, where the decision seems 'close', we might well want to ask how much anguish Brutus' deed would cause. We would want to know how widespread an increase of insecurity and suspicion in Roman society the deed would be likely to produce. To what extent would it encourage other murders? Just what will Brutus' state of mind be like once he has become a murderer? In how much danger are Roman free institutions? To what extent is this an inevitable historical trend, and to what extent could it be checked by the death of Caesar?

The answers to all of these questions are highly relevant to Brutus' decision. Most of them, also, are very difficult to answer. In order to have adequate answers to all of them Brutus would have to have considerable sociological and historical insight, as well as considerable self-knowledge (concerning the effects of murder on his own psychology). This difficulty itself suggests a good reason for not committing the murder. As Moore pointed out, where one is uncertain it is best to do the *kind* of thing which usually is right: in this case abstain from murder.[1]

Suppose however that Brutus claims to be able to judge adequately all of the relevant factors. He is struck by the degree of the damage to free institutions which Caesar has done, by the excellence of the chances for the recovery of these institutions if Caesar leaves the scene, the degree to which brave and public-spirited conduct would be encouraged by the example of his action, etc. On the balance he judges it better to kill Caesar.

Now this may look like a 'textbook' application of Baier's model to an actual moral problem. However there is one crucial difference. Brutus is not saying that the balance of reasons is on the side of killing Caesar. He is saying that the balance of considerations is on the side of killing Caesar.

We can see the point more clearly if we chart the reasons both supporting and opposing Brutus' deed. Such a chart would look something like this.

PRO	CON
Caesar has damaged free institutions.	It would be murder.
There is an excellent chance for the recovery of these institutions if Caesar leaves the scene.	Caesar would lose the pleasure of living.
	Caesar's family and friends would be distressed.
If Brutus killed Caesar, this would encourage brave and public-spirited actions throughout the Roman world.	Brutus' psychological life may be poisoned.
	Violent acts would be encouraged throughout the Roman world.
	It would be ingratitude.

[1] Cf. *Principia Ethica* (Cambridge: Cambridge University Press, 1954), p. 162.

It is important to notice the vagueness of almost all of the statements, on both sides of the page. To say that violent acts would be encouraged throughout the Roman world does not say what kinds of violent acts these might be, to what degree the frequency of violent acts of various kinds would increase. Even if these data were supplied, there still would be considerable vagueness as to the circumstances in which these violent acts might be performed, who the most likely victims might be, etc. To say that Caesar's family and friends would be distressed, to pick another example, also suffers from vagueness: there are very many degrees and kinds of distress, including some to which only Shakespeare could do justice. It is vague also to say that there is an excellent chance for the recovery of free institutions if Caesar leaves the scene: one wants to know which institutions are likely to recover, in what spirit they are likely to operate under a new regime, etc.

None of this is to criticize these pro and con reasons. They are perfectly respectable reasons, and they are as precise as we normally require that reasons in moral argument be. The point is this. There are a great many cases in which a moral choice could be described to us in terms which have this degree of precision, reasons pro and con can be supplied, and we can readily make an intelligent and correct decision. If we are Ann Landers, and someone writes to ask 'Should I abandon my benefactor on a desert island which has an inadequate food supply so that I can have more money with which to buy books?' we do not need a more precise account than this. We do not need to know how quickly the benefactor will starve to death, or what kinds of books the ingrate will buy. However in difficult cases we may well need more than the bare bones of a description. In really difficult cases, it is open to question whether any description will give us all of what we need. For example, if the factors pro and con in the case of Brutus appear very closely matched, it may be extremely important for us to know just how likely it is that free institutions will again flourish if Brutus kills Caesar, and also in what spirit they would be likely to operate. Will they operate in a decadent or ritualistic manner, or will they involve a vigorous awareness of the rights of individuals? Of course there are many varieties of decadence and of ritualistic character, and vigorous awareness of the rights of individuals can take many forms: we may need to know still more. Even further details may not tell us all that we need to know.

It is important to remember that any description that we can

give is general, and thus any description will apply to all of the
cases which share the general features specified by the description.
It is always possible, in really difficult cases, that there may be
morally relevant differences between two cases to which a single,
fairly detailed description applies. It is for this reason, among
others, that it is sometimes very unwise to give moral advice to
people unless one knows them and their problems very well; and
for this reason also it is open to us to conclude that we simply cannot judge what Brutus ought to have done. It is always possible to say
'Unless you were there, you could not fully appreciate the situation'.

Getting back to the lists of reasons pro and con, we can see that,
since after all the reasons are put in general terms, the same sets of
reasons could be produced in a number of cases, some of which
might differ from one another in morally relevant ways. We could
imagine Brutus confronted with two such cases, and deciding that
in one it would be best on the balance to kill Caesar, and that in the
other it would be best on the balance not to kill Caesar. Yet the
lists of reasons would be the same in both cases. Brutus clearly
could not then say that the pro reasons outweigh the con reasons
in one case and not in the other.

It might be objected that I am overlooking a crucial point. If
there are morally relevant differences we can articulate them. For
each morally relevant difference we can add a corresponding reason
to our list, or suitably modify the reasons already on our list.

This *is* a crucial point. This is the focal point of my doubt. My
impression is that some moral problems, such as Brutus', may be
finer than the net of the vocabulary we can use in formulating them.
The vocabulary available to us in dealing with moral problems is
limited, and highly imprecise; the factors relevant to a choice may
be various and subtle.

This may change if the social sciences and history all become
highly developed and precise sciences, with the precise vocabulary
appropriate to such sciences. (Whether they are capable of such a
development is itself a highly complex philosophical issue. As
admirers of Sartre know, there are grounds for scepticism.) Given
such an apparatus, we might be able to approach moral problems
in a precise and semi-scientific manner. In the meantime, though,
it looks different. It does seem highly questionable, for example,
whether we can count on articulating with existing vocabulary all
of the morally relevant features of the effects which Brutus' action
might have on the institutional life of Rome.

Let us suppose that Brutus weighs the relevant factors, as best he can, and decides that the balance inclines very slightly in favour of killing Caesar. It is easy to see the grounds on which he might refuse to relate his choice to a moral principle of more than minimal generality. He might refuse to affirm the principle, for example, that it is right to kill a dictator in cases in which such an action would create an excellent chance for the recovery of free institutions, and would encourage brave and public-spirited actions. He might argue that in some cases of this kind it might well not be right to kill a dictator: various subtle factors might incline the balance the other way. Furthermore, he might refuse to delimit the factors which would be relevant to a moral choice in a case like this. Consequently, he might affirm merely a principle of minimal generality (or what we might call the inarticulate man's substitute for a general principle), namely the statement that a choice like this would be right in any case which would be extremely similar to his in relevant respects. Brutus can affirm that one cannot articulate fully what would count as extreme similarity or which respects are relevant. [We may recall Hare's statement that a moral principle (if one continues to call it that) 'may be so complex that it defies formulation in words at all'.][1] As I have pointed out, this need not prevent us from saying that Brutus' problem was a moral problem, or from saying that he approached it as a moral problem.

The burden of my argument has been that, while Brutus may well weigh considerations in arriving at his moral decision, it would be misleading to describe the process simply as one of weighing reasons. The best decision is the one which is supported by the strongest considerations, but again it seems somewhat misleading to speak of the best decision as that which is supported by the strongest reasons. Of course, if one allows 'This will have the best overall consequences' to enter the list of reasons, it is highly arguable that the best decision will be that which is supported by the strongest reasons. But highly sophisticated judgment, which may well not be merely a matter of weighing reasons, may be required to determine what will have the best overall consequences.[2]

[1] Cf. R. M. Hare, *Freedom and Reason* (Oxford: Oxford University Press, 1963), pp. 39, 40.

[2] My position here may seem to have some affinities to that of the classic 'intuitionists'. A discussion of differences would constitute too great an interruption of the main line of argument. My view is that, if there is any useful role in ethical theory for the concept of intuition, it is as a limiting concept. If one

The third point at which I am inclined to be doubtful of Baier's view involves his claim that 'Moral deliberation . . . is a sort of calculus. . . . All that can be expected of moral philosophers is the clarification of this calculus, the statement of the general rules, and the methods of using them in particular calculations.'[1] Baier elsewhere rejects the view 'that there is not and cannot be a proper, absolutely definitive, method for normative ethics'.[2] He is keenly aware that some moral problems are made difficult by conflicting considerations and conflicting reasons. He speaks of 'rules of priority', which we take from our 'social environment', which one uses in weighing facts relevant to a case.[3] He also speaks of 'rules of superiority', which enable us to weigh the merits of conflicting reasons.[4]

I have already indicated one reason for scepticism here. To speak of moral deliberation as 'a sort of calculus' is to make moral deliberation sound much more precise than it usually is. In addition to this, to speak of 'rules of priority' and 'rules of superiority' is to make it seem that moral reasoning generally follows much neater and more definite logical patterns than it does. Fully articulated 'rules of priority' and 'rules of superiority' are the dream of the casuist: nowadays if a philosopher speaks of them, a thoughtful man will want to see the philosopher's list.

It is true that most of us do take 'rules of priority', at least of a rough and crude sort, from our environment. It is thus that we get our ideas that murder is more heinous than theft, and that in general we prefer the preservation of lives to the preservation of property. But it is worth pointing out that we do not all accept the same 'rules of priority'. Some people, in surveying Brutus' problem, might argue simply that the preservation of free institutions does not justify a single act of violence; other people might argue that if Brutus' act really were going clearly to have a major effect of restoring free institutions it would be justified. A somewhat similar conflict concerning priorities is crudely embodied in the 'Better dead than red' controversy. Even if we get rules of

---

wished, one could speak of a conclusion as having been reached partly by means of intuition, meaning simply that it had not been reached entirely by means of reason.

[1] *The Moral Point of View*, p. 172.
[2] 'Fact, Value, and Norm in Stevenson's Ethics', *Nous*, Vol. 1 (1967), p. 156.
[3] *The Moral Point of View*, p. 106.
[4] *ibid.*, p. 170.

priority from our social environment, the social environment speaks with many voices.

Baier in fact has suggested (if I read him rightly) that proper application of the moral calculus might eliminate the cold war.[1] I myself am inclined to agree with his moral viewpoint here; but some very intelligent, 'well-meaning', and (by most standards) moral people would not. This is part of the problem.

Here, as at so many other places in this book, I may seem to be arguing on the side of the subjectivist. In these places I want to say 'The subjectivist has a point'. To speak of moral deliberation as a calculus, and to speak as Baier does of rules of priority, is to gloss over those deep differences which make moral debate sometimes so difficult. This is not to deny that some rules of priority are, at least roughly, correct. I myself am prepared to argue that, in making any moral choice concerning nuclear war, we should consider the virtual annihilation of the human race to be more disastrous than its existence under a totalitarian regime; I am prepared to argue that anyone who feels differently is simply wrong. But my claim, strictly speaking, is incapable of proof; and it would be question-begging in the extreme to argue against my opponent simply on the grounds that he has misread the social environment. He would be wrong even if his rule of priority were learned by everyone at his mother's knee.

The difficulty for Baier can be put this way. Suppose that we are in a situation in which there are only two alternatives. Either we surrender to a fascist dictatorship (a Mussolini brown shirt affair), or we engage in a nuclear war which will destroy at least ninety-five per cent of the world's population. In practice, of course, we do not expect to be limited to two such alternatives, which is one of the things which makes the 'Better dead than red' controversy so childish. But suppose that we really have only these two alternatives. I argue that we ought to accept the fascist dictatorship ('Better fascism than the destruction of human society', I say); my opponent argues that we ought rather to embrace nuclear war ('Better dead than brown', he says). We clearly have conflicting rules of priority. The question for Baier is 'Where is the rule which will decide between our rules?' Baier may of course propose a super-rule which will do this, but if my opponent then proposes a conflicting super-rule, where is the super-rule which will decide

[1] Cf. 'Moral Obligation', *American Philosophical Quarterly*, Vol. 3 (1966), p. 226.

between these super-rules? It is easy to see how questions like these can be answered, but it is not easy to see how they can be settled.

III

Most of my criticism of Toulmin and Baier has not involved frontal assaults on their positions. Indeed it should be clear to the reader that the tendency of this chapter has been more towards agreement than disagreement. My major doubts are centred more on the pictures of ethical reasoning which Toulmin and Baier encourage (by their points of emphasis and omissions) than on their specific claims. It is not my purpose to develop a full-fledged account of the role of reason in ethics which is very sharply different from Toulmin's and Baier's.

Two points about the role of reason in ethics are however worth developing. When these two points have been developed, I shall have defined my position more thoroughly regarding the cognitive role of reason in ethics.

First, the most basic assertion which Toulmin and Baier both make clearly is correct. Reason does play a part in ethics: both in arriving at and in justifying ethical judgments. The man who is tempted to abandon his benefactor on a desert island may reason that the harm to his benefactor outweighs the advantages to himself, and may accordingly decide that he should not abandon his benefactor. The man who needs medicine for his desperately ill children may reason that society owes them the chance to live, that his stealing from a rich man will create less harm than the good it will produce for his children, and accordingly may decide that he is morally justified in committing a minor theft.

Many philosophers have stressed the fact that reason may not carry conviction. We have perhaps a greater capacity to be wilfully blind in moral matters than in matters of any other kind. Thus the man who is tempted to abandon his benefactor on a desert island may simply ignore the arguments against his action, or may 'rationalize'. The man who needs medicine for his desperately ill children, who lives in a thoroughly uncharitable society, may through timidity also 'rationalize', and decide that stealing is always wrong, even in the most extreme case. Alternatively, a man whose needs are much less desperate, and who does live in a fairly charitable society, may claim that his case is much more like that of the man with desperately ill children than it really is, and thus 'rationalize' his desire to steal from people whose need is almost as great as his.

When all is said, however, perhaps the most amazing thing is that reason sometimes does carry conviction. Men sometimes can be argued out of courses of action which they very much want to pursue. Good reasons, carefully presented, sometimes can convince men not to commit acts of theft, murder, etc. which they have been inclined to commit.

How much of a correlation there is between the strength of reasons and their persuasive capacity is a psychological question. There is a related logical point, however. A good reason is a good reason even if it has no persuasive capacity; a bad reason is a bad reason even if it has very great persuasive capacity. If a man wants to steal from a shopkeeper, to say that theft may cause suffering to the shopkeeper, and will encourage insecurity and suspicion within society, is a good reason against the theft even if it influences no one. I think that almost everyone would agree that it would be a good reason even if (through some mass hypnosis) everyone were to scoff at it. Conversely, I think that everyone would consider 'The possibility of theft would make everyone more alert during working hours' a poor reason in support of a theft, even under the hypothesis that mass hypnosis were to make everyone receptive to this reason. Also 'It would preserve freedom' is not a very good reason for choosing nuclear war, even if many people think that it is.

Of course there are differences of opinion—in some cases one wants to say 'legitimate differences'—concerning the strength of reasons. There is a virtual consensus in our society that 'It encourages insecurity and suspicion' is a good reason against theft, and for that matter against murder, and that 'It relieves pain with few difficulties for oneself' is a good reason for being charitable to people who are starving. There is much less consensus over how good a reason 'It would do more good for them than for you' is for giving a third of one's salary to the poor, or over how good a reason 'It would make them self-reliant' is for making all able-bodied men who are on welfare work on special projects.

There appears to be a continuum with regard to the certainty about the strength of a reason which most people feel is justified. Most people would regard someone who persistently maintained that 'The possibility of theft would make everyone more alert during working hours' was a good reason in support of a theft, in somewhat the same light as they would regard the man (in Chapter

IV) who persistently claims (despite all of the evidence which we present) that there is an elephant in the room. Such a man is simply unreasonable (even if, strictly speaking, we cannot *prove* him wrong). At the other extreme, even someone who does not consider 'It would do more good for them than for you' a very strong reason for giving one-third of one's salary to the poor, may well hesitate to consider as ridiculous or foolish someone who does consider it a very strong reason. Here, we might say, there is more room for argument. Reasonable men may differ. 'It would do more good for them than for you', as a reason for giving two-thirds of one's income to the poor, might be argued to be a case intermediate between the two extremes. Many people would feel that there is more room for argument here than in the case in which theft was justified by virtue of promoting alertness, but perhaps not as much room as in the case in which one-third of one's salary was at stake.

Even in the case of 'It would do more good for them than for you', as a reason for giving one-third of one's salary to the poor, the strength of the reason would not be generally interpreted as a subjective matter. Most of us would say 'Do what you think is right'; but only someone in the grip of a philosophical theory would say 'If you think that it is a strong reason it is; if you think that it is not a strong reason it is not', or would interpret saying that the reason is strong to be simply a reflection of one's attitude and nothing more. A more normal response, I think, would be to say instead simply that the problem is difficult, and that we are not sure of (or do not know) the answer. Or we might say that we think that the reason is (or is not) a strong reason, but that we might well be wrong. Many people are willing to say, with regard to very difficult ethical questions, that they might be wrong.

Thus it is clear that there are good reasons and poor reasons in ethics, but in some cases it is not entirely clear how good a reason is. This is one of the factors which makes the logic of ethical argument so complicated and difficult.

The second point about the role of reason in ethics which I wish to develop is this. Reason often plays an important part in arriving at ethical judgments, but in some cases it plays very little part. The average man knows, without any explicit reasoning process, that he should not kill his enemy or steal from the neighbourhood supermarket. Reason also may play very little part in B's judgment (in the previous chapter) that Mr X's life was empty. B simply 'saw' this. He could have reasoned about the matter, starting with certain assumptions about what counts as an 'empty' life; but he did not have to.

Two factors which may co-operate with reason, or in some cases pre-empt the need for reason, are authority and experience. It is probable that most people believe on the basis of authority that they should not murder their enemies, and have not 'reasoned' it out. In some cases, though, someone who accepts the wrongness of murder on authority may not realize that a specific act (e.g. abandoning his benefactor on a desert island) would be murder; and here reason, by making clear to him the character of the act, co-operates with authority. Reason also may help to extend moral principles beyond what authority has provided: reason may tell a man that imprisoning debtors causes suffering in much the same way as do other actions which he already considers immoral, and thus may convince him that imprisoning debtors too is morally wrong.

A man need not reason things out to know that a life of complete idleness is not highly desirable: he may arrive at the answer simply by trying such a life. Or he may reason that, in his experience, the deepest satisfactions have come from reaching goals for which he has striven, that an idle life would be essentially without goals, and that consequently such a life would not be desirable.

A detailed examination of the various uses of reason, authority, and experience in arriving at ethical judgments would itself be the matter of an entire book. In terms of an argument that there is ethical knowledge, however, the major points have been made. The rational character of ethics has been re-stated, but not overstated.

How tempting it has been to overstate the rational character of ethics can be seen if we reflect on the dilemma with which Ayer left philosophers. Unless one firmly and clearly rejected Ayer's assumptions, there were only two grounds on which one could argue that ethics was 'cognitive'. One was the ground that ethical judgments really were empirically verifiable. This however seemed quite implausible, in view of Moore's arguments against naturalistic ethics, and in view also of the stubborn character of so much ethical disagreement. The other ground was that ethics really was a kind of logic. Reason clearly does play an important role in ethics, and arguably most ethical arguments do not fit the patterns of old-fashioned logic texts. Thus it was very tempting for philosophers to emphasize the role of reason in ethics, examine its distinctive features, but make it seem simpler or neater than it is, and ignore other factors involved in arriving at ethical judgments. This would tend to establish ethics as 'cognitive', even on Ayer's terms; but it is too simple a way out.

Ethics is not a kind of logic. It is not only that, as H. D. Aiken has pointed out, 'it is far more appropriate to say that it is false that I ought to beat my grandmother than to say that it is invalid'.[1] It is not only that it seems, in practice, impossible to discover the correctness of some complicated ethical claims (e.g. 'A life centred entirely on wealth and fame is not highly desirable') entirely, as it were, *a priori*. It is also that ethical reasoning requires principles or assumptions which, on one hand, few would care to regard simply as arbitrarily chosen axioms, and which, on the other hand, cannot themselves be based entirely on reason. As Toulmin pointed out, a good deal of ethical reasoning involves locating an action as forbidden or required by the code of one's society. Most people who engage in reasoning of this kind presumably accept the code on the basis of authority. Toulmin felt that a code could be justified (if in fact it was justifiable) in terms of social harmony. But on what basis do we determine that social harmony is good? At the foundations we may be driven to appeal to something like Hume's sentiment of benevolence; whatever it is that we appeal to, the fact remains that substantive ethical claims (e.g. 'It is better that people live than die', or 'Pain is bad'—both things that anyone who has lived and felt pain is in a position to know) must lie at the foundation of any ethical reasoning, and that rational justification has to end somewhere short of the foundation. Every fundamental claim, even that pain is bad, is subject to question. Thus any suggestion that ethical knowledge can be based entirely on reason appears very implausible.

[1] *Reason and Conduct* (New York: Alfred A. Knopf, 1962), p. 96.

CHAPTER VIII

THE EXISTENCE OF
ETHICAL KNOWLEDGE

Is there ethical knowledge? For seven chapters we have circled around this question, discussing the views of philosophers such as Moore, Ayer, and Stevenson, and also examining the roles of experience and reason in ethics. We now can confront the central question.

In Chapter I, I distinguished two aspects which my central argument must have. One involves an appeal to our ordinary ethical discourse; the other involves the defensive argument that there are no overriding philosophical or ethical reasons for rejecting the 'cognitivism' argued to be implicit in ordinary language. Both aspects already have been developed to some extent. In Chapter III, I appealed to the implications of our ordinary ethical discourse in arguing against Stevenson. In Chapter IV, and again in Chapter VI, I laid the groundwork of an argument (against Ayer) that there are no overriding philosophical reasons for rejecting the thesis that there is ethical knowledge. In Chapter V, and also some remarks at the end of Chapter III, I laid the groundwork of an argument that there are no overriding ethical reasons for rejecting the thesis that there is ethical knowledge.

What we have so far is mainly groundwork. We can pursue the argument now by means of two approaches. One is the approach through examples. If we can produce examples of ethical knowledge, then there is ethical knowledge. An analogue to this is the procedure of the philosopher who argues that material objects exist by arguing that his hands exist. Such an argument can carry great weight, at least in creating a presumption in favour of a position; although to someone from an opposite philosophical camp it can seem infuriatingly simple-minded.

The second approach is through fundamentals. We can ask what knowledge is, being careful not to answer our question with anything so simple as a definition. Having unveiled at least slightly the concept of knowledge, we can ask whether there is anything which is irreducibly ethical (i.e. not immediately transferable to psychology, sociology, logic, etc.) which belongs under the concept of knowledge. We can, as it were, scrutinize the family resemblances of what purports to be ethical knowledge. This will help to construct defences against philosophical objections to my thesis. It also is relevant to ethical objections, since it gives a clearer picture of the weight of what would have to be ignored or modified if we were to abandon a 'cognitivist' way of speaking.

I

Let us begin with the first approach. I shall propose four examples of ethical knowledge, three uncontroversial and one somewhat controversial.

Example 1. Jones has been taught since early childhood that it is in general wrong to steal. He assents, and when questioned says that theft is in general wrong. He has an excellent opportunity to steal an art object which he greatly covets, under conditions in which it is virtually certain that he would escape detection. But he clenches his teeth, for a moment looks like Immanuel Kant, and does not do the deed. (Jones knows that he should not steal the art object.)

Example 2. Smith lives in a society in which it is established practice to imprison debtors. Brown owes Smith a great deal of money, and has responded in an obnoxious manner to Smith's attempts to get the money back. Smith is very much inclined to order Brown's imprisonment. However Smith always has condemned theft, flogging of schoolboys, uncharitable behaviour towards the poor, etc. on the ground that all of these things produce avoidable suffering. He reflects that if Brown is imprisoned both Brown and Brown's family will suffer. He concludes reluctantly that he ought not to order Brown's imprisonment, and in fact desists. (Smith knows that he ought not to have Brown imprisoned.)

Example 3. Green has an air of frivolity, and talks rather lightly about the attractiveness of stealing a great deal of money; in fact he once or twice has stolen very small items from the local supermarket. He has never been in a position to steal a great deal of money. White, who is a skilled psychologist, notices that Green, despite his frivolous talk, works steadily at his studies, and writes regularly to his aged mother. He concludes that Green is not really a bad person. Later Green has an opportunity to commit a major theft, under extremely favourable circumstances, and refuses. (White knows that Green is not really a bad person.)

Example 4. Black is independently wealthy, and has had the opportunity to sample a number of ways of life. He has lived in complete idleness for a while, and for a while has plunged into frenetic pleasure-seeking. He has found both ways of life not very satisfying. He also has tried a life devoted primarily to learning, with a great deal of time spent in hard thought on intellectually challenging problems. This way of life makes Black feel much more 'fulfilled'; he also feels that in this way of life he pays less in boredom and frustration for his moments of pleasure. He concludes that a very highly desirable life, at least for those who are capable of it, is one which involves a great deal of well-conducted contemplative activity. (Black knows that a well-conducted contemplative life is highly desirable.)

The first example is of a case in which someone might claim to have knowledge based on authority. A salient feature is the relation between knowledge and action. It would be possible for Jones to yield to temptation, and yet for us to say that Jones knew that what he did was wrong. However, as I pointed out in my discussion of hypocrisy in Chapter II, if Jones were to yield extremely easily to temptation (manifesting no scruples, no guilt, no especial desire to avoid committing theft) we would be inclined to deny that he really believed (or knew) that he should not steal. If, when Jones resolutely rejects the temptation to steal, we are convinced that Jones knows that it would be wrong to steal the art object, it is partly that we believe that the authority of society (regarding the wrongness of theft) is here thoroughly reliable (so that we believe that Jones is right, and has a right to be confident), and partly that Jones convinces us by his actions that he really believes that it would be wrong to steal the art object.

The second example is one in which we would be inclined to speak of knowledge as based on reason. We would tend to say, that is, that reason has enabled Smith to know that he ought not to order Brown's imprisonment. The reasoning is of a type common in ethics: we find the basis of some of our moral judgments (in Smith's case, the belief that in general one should not act so as to cause avoidable suffering), and then apply this to a fresh case. It is widely recognized that this type of reasoning may give major support to its conclusion: we would be inclined to say that Smith's conclusion about imprisoning Brown has a much better basis here than it would have if Smith had decided not to imprison Brown because legal proceedings are unlucky, or because Brown's imprisonment would diminish the number of people able to play the national lottery. Yet no one would confuse Smith's reasoning with proof. R. M. Hare gives another way in which Smith could arrive at his conclusion by means of reasoning: Smith could ask whether, if it were the case that he owed someone money, he then ought to be imprisoned. It follows from the universalizability principle that, unless he can claim that there are relevant differences, if he judges that he should not be imprisoned if he owed money, he is then logically committed to judging that Brown should not be imprisoned.[1] This reasoning too does not *prove* that Smith ought not to have Brown imprisoned. Smith may, after all, fanatically decide that if he were in Brown's position he ought to be imprisoned; he then can consistently decide that he ought to imprison Brown.[2]

The third example is one in which we would be inclined to speak of knowledge as based on experience. It is like Example 1 in Chapter VI. Here too, if we speak of White as knowing that Green is really not a bad person, a large part of what we are suggesting is that White is in an especially good position to make predictions. We are suggesting, that is, that White's observations, combined with the expertise which he brings to his observations, give him a right to be confident of the predictions which he makes of Green's behaviour. The right to be confident of these predictions is closely allied to, but not inseparable from, the right to be confident of a judgment of Green's character. I have already indicated, in Chapter VI, some of the conditions under which we might grant White the right to be confident of his predictions, but refuse him the right to be confident of his judgment of character. White may be prejudiced against Green in some way, or may have standards or tendencies of judgment of which we think very little. Barring some such factor, if we grant White the right to be confident of his predictions, we are very likely to grant him the right to be confident of his judgment of character.

The fourth example is of a case which is somewhat more controversial than the first three, at least in relation to prevailing ideologies. More people would be inclined to dispute Black's con-

---

[1] Cf. *Freedom and Reason* (Oxford: Oxford University Press, 1963), p. 90ff.
[2] Cf. *ibid.*, p. 110.

clusion here than would be inclined to dispute Jones' judgment that he should not steal, Smith's judgment that it is wrong to imprison Brown, or the character judgments of a skilled psychologist. Yet Black's conclusion here is a toned-down version of a classic point in ethical philosophy: it bears resemblances to conclusions arrived at by Plato, Aristotle and Spinoza, among others. I have toned the conclusion down partly because of my own pluralistic tendency to believe that there are a number of ways of life, including those of a highly creative composer, artist, poet, or statesman (or even that of a mystically attuned warrior, cf. the *Bhagavad Gita*), which can compete with the contemplative life.

Those of us who accept Black's conclusion, and who would claim that someone who had fairly tried a variety of ways of life would virtually have to come to Black's conclusion, would be inclined to say that Black knows through experience that a contemplative life is desirable. As I pointed out in Chapter VI, in this kind of case 'experience' may have a very personal quality. Someone may be exposed to the same events and routines as Black, and yet experience something very different.

I wish now to develop two points about these four examples. One is that in each case we would normally be inclined to say that the ethical claim involved was correct (or incorrect), or that the ethical conclusion was right (or wrong), or (if we regard the issues in sufficient abstraction from our dispositions and the dispositions of the people involved) that what was being proposed was true (or false). Thus we would normally be inclined to say that Jones was right in judging that he ought not to steal the art object; we normally would regard it as correct to say that theft is in general wrong.

As I indicated earlier, what is crucial is not the fact that we are prepared to use words like 'right', 'correct' and 'true' in speaking of ethical judgments, but rather the gloss that we are prepared to put on this fact. The gloss that almost everyone not in the grip of a special philosophical theory would be inclined to put, I think, is as follows. When we say that Jones' ethical judgment is correct, we mean that this is the case independently of what he or anyone else (including us) thinks. We would be prepared to say that his judgment would be correct even if he were somehow convinced no longer to make it, and we and everyone else were convinced somehow no longer to agree to it. If it is correct, then it is correct independently of all of these circumstances. If we agree with the ethical judgments of Smith, White and Black, we presumably would be prepared to say the same thing about their judgments.

Now it is possible to interpret our ascription of correctness here as 're-iterative': this certainly is defensible as part of a theory of truth (and correctness) which regards the use of 'true' (and 'correct') generally as reiterative. But it is important to keep in mind that when we say that Jones' judgment is correct, we are not simply reporting or expressing our agreement. We are making the claim that, even if we were not to agree, Jones' judgment would be correct. In a sense we *are* repeating Jones' judgment: that is, we too are asserting that it *would* be wrong for him to steal the art object.

The second point is simply that the word 'know' is at home in these cases. It is natural to say that Jones knows that he should not steal the art object, that Smith knows that he should not imprison Brown, and that White knows that Green is not really a bad person. There may be some difficulty with regard to the claim that Black knows that a contemplative life is highly desirable, but the difficulty is due mainly, I think, to the controversial character of Black's decision. Anyone who is firmly convinced that Black is right would not find it odd to say that Black knows from experience the desirability of a contemplative life. (Compare 'You know that it is awful to work twelve hours a day on an assembly line' with 'You know that it is much better to have peace of mind than to be continually worried about things'.)

Here again the gloss that we are prepared to put on our use of a word is as important as the fact that we use the word. It sometimes is argued that, when we use 'know' in ethical cases, the knowledge of which we speak is really psychological, sociological, or legal knowledge. It is important to see how true this is.

There is at least a grain of truth in this claim. Consider for example what may well be the most common sense in which we speak of people as 'knowing right from wrong'. This is the legal sense.[1] In the legal sense, as long as a man is sane and familiar with the mores and laws of our society, he knows that murder is wrong, even if he is a hardened killer who kills cheerfully, never hesitates,

---

[1] My distinction between ethical and legal senses of 'knowing' what is right and wrong is one which I failed to make in 'Nuance and Ethical Choice' (*Ethics*, January 1969). However I still stand by the major argument of that essay: namely that there are good reasons for rejecting a model of ethical judgment which is implicit in much of our ordinary ethical discourse. This may go to prove that I do have a liberal streak with regard to ordinary language.

never feels guilt, etc. If one asks *what* it is which the hardened killer (who 'knows that murder is wrong') knows, the obvious answer is in terms of the legal and moral classification which has been given to acts of murder. (That a moral as well as a legal classification is involved can be argued as follows. We know that it is illegal to park in a 'no parking' area, but we would not normally say that we knew that it was wrong. This suggests that knowing merely that something is legally prohibited is not sufficient to speak of 'knowing that it is wrong'.) Thus the legal sense of 'knowing' that murder is wrong appears closely related to the sociological sense of 'knowing' that murder is wrong, in which what is known is the moral attitude of society towards murder.

It is important to realize that the sociological sense of 'belief' and 'knowledge' in ethics is parasitic. That is, it is impossible to know (or be in a position to have beliefs about) what is generally believed right and wrong unless people have performed the primary activity of believing certain things right and wrong. Similarly, while it is possible for an individual to 'know' in the legal sense that murder is wrong without himself believing it (in the sense of having a fairly strong disposition to avoid committing murders), it is not possible for anyone to 'know' in the legal sense that murder is wrong unless we already have some general concept of moral wrongness (which involves people believing that certain things are wrong in a sense which involves having a fairly strong disposition not to do these things). (This does not of course conflict with the theory that among some primitive peoples law and morals are intertwined, so that only at a fairly advanced stage are some things considered immoral but not illegal, or illegal but not immoral.) Thus both the legal and the sociological senses of 'knowing' what is right and wrong presuppose what I regard as the irreducibly ethical sense: namely one which requires a fairly strong disposition to act in accordance with what one is said to know.

One difficulty in disentangling the legal and sociological senses of 'knowing that murder is wrong' from the ethical sense is that we normally assume that sane adults who know the moral code of our society really have some reluctance to commit murders (even if temptations overcome that reluctance). Conversely, if it becomes crystal clear that a man has no reluctance at all, we are inclined on that ground alone to wonder either about his sanity or about whether anyone communicated to him the moral code of our society. Still let us formulate the following case. Z is greatly tempted to murder a lout of his acquaintance. He is genuinely inclined to think that he should commit the murder (the lout has no redeeming features, and is in his way). Now of course he knows that murder is condemned in our society, and in that sense and in a legal sense he knows that murder is wrong. But does he know that murder is wrong in the sense in which you have really to believe that murder is wrong in order to know it? ('Really believing' in this context of course involves a fairly strong disposition not to commit murders.) I believe that most people would be able to recognize the sense about which we are asking, and would judge that in this sense Z perhaps does not know that murder is wrong. Indeed if we said to Z himself, while he was inclined to feel that he really should kill the lout 'You know that murder is wrong', he might well reply 'I know no such thing'.

The sense in which Z's inclinations and pronouncements would incline us (and him) to doubt that he knows that murder is wrong is a purely ethical sense. It plainly is not a sociological or a legal sense, since in those senses Z clearly does know that murder is wrong.

The knowledge in question also is distinct from psychological knowledge. First, Z may know perfectly well what his feelings and attitudes are (and thus have psychological knowledge), and yet have attitudes so ambivalent that he correctly says that he does not know whether murder is wrong or not. Secondly, let us suppose that Z does decide that murder is wrong, and that he now thoroughly disapproves of it. The claim that Z knows that he thoroughly disapproves of murder (which is psychological knowledge) does not logically entail the claim that Z knows that murder is wrong. We can see this if we examine the case in which Ezra Pound knows that he thoroughly disapproves of banks' charging interest on loans. We might credit Pound here with psychological knowledge, but this does not commit us to saying that he knows that it is wrong for banks to charge interest on loans. Once we see this, we see that in order to infer 'Z knows that murder is wrong' (in an ethical sense) from 'Z knows that he thoroughly disapproves of murder' we need additional premises: the premise that Z's judgment is correct, and the premise that Z somehow has a right to be confident of his judgment. (We shall discuss these conditions for ethical knowledge shortly.) Thus the knowledge with which we might decide to credit Z, in the sense of 'knowing that murder is wrong' which we are discussing, cannot be identified with psychological knowledge.

In Example 1, Jones, if he knows the laws and the prevailing moral attitudes towards theft, and knows his own attitudes, presumably has legal, sociological, and psychological knowledge. But in order for us to credit him with 'knowing' in an ethical sense that he should not steal the art object, he must also really believe that he should not steal it; we also must agree with his judgment, and agree that he makes it on good authority (or in some other way has a right to be confident).

The irreducibly ethical sense of 'know' has sharper outlines in the other three examples, especially since there is no competing legal sense. In the case of Brown and Smith, under our hypothesis the laws of the realm permitted Smith to imprison Brown, so that if we speak (as we normally would) of Smith as knowing that he ought not to imprison Brown, we are scarcely using 'know' in a legal sense. If there is no strong pattern of social disapproval of someone who imprisons debtors, then Smith's knowledge cannot be interpreted as sociological. The argument given in the case of murder would show also that Smith's knowledge that he should not imprison Brown cannot be identified with psychological knowledge.

In the case of White knowing that Green is not really a bad person, there would be a case for interpreting White's knowledge as sociological, i.e. as knowledge of how Green would be rated in relation to socially endorsed ethical standards. Indeed, if White agrees with socially endorsed ethical standards it may be very difficult for him to distinguish between the sociological and ethical characters of his claim: the two may seem inseparable in his mind, so to speak. However we can ask whether he feels committed by his judgment of Green to judge that Green is not really bad even in the following case. We suppose that the standards of society radically change so that providing for one's family is considered far more important than the property 'rights' of others. Theft is considered illegal but not immoral. Successful thieves who support their families very well are considered good men; unsuccessful thieves and people who refuse obviously good chances to commit a successful theft are considered 'bad'. We suppose further that Green, as before, refuses an excellent opportunity to commit successfully a major theft. Now if White says 'Given these facts, I judge that Green would be bad', it looks very much as if his original judgment really had a sociological character, and as if the knowledge that it embodied has to be interpreted as sociological rather than ethical knowledge. (We would not be entirely sure of this, however. It is possible for White to maintain that a change in society's attitudes is an important morally relevant difference between the present case of Green and the hypothetical case of Green. We have to ascertain whether White's judgments are simply a function of what the attitude of society would be or not.) However, White may reply instead, 'Even in that case I judge that Green would not really be bad: indeed he would be right, and the prevalent opinion of society would be wrong.' Then it looks very much as if his original judgment really had an ethical character, and as if the knowledge it embodied has to be interpreted as ethical rather than sociological knowledge.

There is one obvious objection to this which I should meet. It may be objected that, when we ask White what he would consider an appropriate judgment if . . ., even though we are hypothesizing changed sociological conditions, the sociological conditions under which White answers our question are of course the ones under which he made his original judgment. His answer may well continue to reflect these conditions, even if we have been hypothesizing changed conditions.

It is important, however, to distinguish between a judgment's being *about* sociological conditions, and a judgment's *reflecting* sociological conditions. It may well be that only moral reformers, or men who ethically are 'ahead of' (or behind, or radically apart from) their time make ethical judgments which do not reflect the accepted standards of their society. But to say that Z's judgment, that it is wrong to kill a lout who stands in your way, for example, reflects the standards of our society is not to say that Z's judgment is about the standards of our society. If Z's judgment turns out indeed to be about the standards of our society, then of course it is a sociological judgment, and is not what I have called irreducibly ethical. But if Z's judgment is that it is wrong to kill the lout even if society were to happen to approve of cleverly executed killing of louts, then his judgment cannot be interpreted as being about the standards of society. It may well be that the causes of his making the judgment may be analysed sociologically, but this is not to say that his judgment is about something sociological.

Let us return to the case of White and Green. Even if the causes of White's judgment may be interpreted sociologically (e.g. 'A middle-class psychologist imbued with the standards of our society may be expected to respond in such and such a manner to such and such a case'), if White's judgment applies independently of what established ethical standards happen to be, then White's judgment is irreducibly ethical and not sociological. It also is not psychological. White's judgment is closely related to psychological judgments (those involved in predicting Green's behaviour); but, as I pointed out, it is distinct. It is possible for White's psychological judgments of Green to be correct, and yet for his ethical judgment to be wrong. For example, if White is highly prejudiced against Green, he may correctly predict Green's behaviour, and yet judge that Green is much worse than he is.

It would be difficult to interpret as sociological Black's claim to know that a contemplative life is highly desirable. It might be more plausible to interpret it as psychological, since, in a sense, it is a claim about what in the long run will be satisfying. Indeed, as I pointed out in Chapter I, the line between a value-ridden psychology and some parts of ethics may be very blurred. However, if Black is prepared to claim that a highly contemplative life is more desirable than a life devoted to pleasure-seeking even for an intelligent man who really prefers a life of pleasure-seeking, his claim looks much more ethical than psychological. If we are prepared to claim that he has knowledge, the knowledge would have to be classified as ethical. If (as I would assert) Books I and X of the *Nichomachean Ethics* express important knowledge, this knowledge on the whole would have to be considered irreducibly ethical.

Let me sum up the results of our first approach. We have seen that we normally often speak of ethical claims as correct and incorrect, in a way such that correctness cannot be interpreted merely in relation to the psychological state or sociological milieu of the person making an ethical claim. We have seen that, in a variety of cases, we normally speak of people who make ethical claims as 'knowing' that which they claim. Sometimes, in such cases, 'know' is used in a sense which must be interpreted as legal or sociological. I have argued however that sometimes 'know' is used in a sense which cannot be interpreted as legal or sociological; and that on these occasions the knowledge which we attribute is distinct from legal, sociological, or psychological knowledge. In short, ordinary usage contains the concept of irreducibly ethical knowledge, and the concept finds use. This creates a *prima facie* strong case for saying that there is ethical knowledge.

To put the point more succinctly, Smith may know that he ought not to imprison Brown, even if he lives in a society in which imprisoning debtors is legal and is not generally condemned, and even if his judgment is that it would be wrong to imprison Brown even though he (Smith) might feel otherwise. If, under these conditions, Smith knows that he ought not to imprison Brown, then of course there is ethical knowledge.

II

The obvious rejoinder is (1) that ordinary usage may be confused, and (2) that our tendency to use 'know' in an irreducibly ethical sense in ethical cases may disappear (as 'non-cognitivist' ethical philosophies influence our language habits), thus undermining my case. In order to deal with these points, we have to get behind the surface facts of ordinary usage. We must ask about knowledge, and how closely related what we now tend to call 'knowledge' (in an ethical sense) in ethical cases is to what we call knowledge in other kinds of cases.

There are of course many kinds of knowledge. There is knowledge which centres on a practical skill, e.g. knowing how to swim, knowing how to read Braille. There is some similarity between what we speak of as 'knowing' in ethical cases and this kind of 'knowing': in both, 'knowledge' has a clear relation to performance. Just as the major test of whether Smith knows how to swim involves observing Smith's performance when (under normal conditions) he tries to swim, part of the test of whether Smith knows (in an ethical sense) that he ought not to imprison Brown for debt involves observing Smith's performance when we give him an excellent opportunity to imprison Brown for debt. Indeed it is a truism to say that ethical 'knowledge' is practical, that it guides conduct and normally to some extent is reflected in conduct.

Nevertheless, the similarity between ethical 'knowing' and 'knowing' which centres on a practical skill is not very great. What Smith says about his performances plays a much greater part in the test for ethical knowledge than in the test for whether Smith knows how to swim or knows how to read Braille. A man's ability to provide reason and argument frequently strengthens the case for saying that he 'knows' in an ethical sense; in the case of most kinds of practical skill, reason and argument do not play a comparable role. Furthermore, knowing that it is wrong to imprison debtors simply is not a skill in the sense that knowing how to swim or read Braille is. A man may know how to swim, and yet have a very strong constant aversion to swimming, so that he never swims. A man may know how to read Braille, and yet dislike it so that he always deliberately misreads what is set before him. But if a man has a very strong constant aversion to letting his debtors stay out of jail, so that he repeatedly has them imprisoned, we would hesitate to say that he really believes, or that in an ethical sense he knows, that he ought not to imprison his debtors. We may say that he is able not to imprison his debtors, but clearly more is required here than an ability.

Another kind of knowledge is that exemplified by knowing what it is like to be locked up for hours in a small windowless room, or knowing what it is like to be exhausted during an attempt to swim the English Channel. Here the major requirement is to have had an experience, although not just any experience: if we asked someone 'Do you know what it is like to be locked up for hours in a small windowless room?' and he replied 'Yes, that happened to me once: I thoroughly enjoyed it', we might not know what to say. Plainly our ability to talk about what happened in the right way, or at least not to talk about it in the wrong way, is relevant to this kind of knowing. It has some obvious similarity to some kinds of ethical knowledge, e.g. 'knowing' that it is awful to work in an assembly line for twelve hours at a time, 'knowing' how undesirable a life devoted entirely to pleasure-seeking can be.

Yet there are obvious major differences. Let me point out one. This is that in the ethical cases someone who has had experiences explicitly places a value on them: presumably the 'knowledge' is of the value of the experiences, and having had the experiences may give one the 'right to be confident' of one's judgment of their value. Because a value is attributed, it is open to us to challenge a person's claim to knowledge simply by saying that the claim of value that he makes is wrong. For example, if someone says 'I know how dreary even a well-conducted contemplative life is', we can say 'You know no such thing', simply on the basis that what he claims to know is wrong. If someone says 'I know what it is like to lead a contemplative life', we may challenge his claim to knowledge, but not on the basis that what he has claimed to know is in fact wrong: he has not claimed to know anything which may be right or wrong.

A third kind of knowledge is knowledge that something is the case, e.g. knowing that Hartford is the capital of Connecticut, that six is the square-root of thirty-six, that the bird outside of my window is a goldfinch. This is the kind of knowledge that lies at the heart of what most philosophers have in mind when they use the word 'cognitive'. In particular this is the kind of knowledge which we associate most closely with the sciences, mathematics, and logic (although of course mastery of any of these subjects involves skills).

My argument will be that what we normally speak of as 'knowing' in an ethical sense has a close similarity to knowledge that something is the case. A word of caution is in order before I begin this argument. To establish this similarity is *not* to argue for an interpretation of ethical knowledge as knowledge that something is the case. Resemblance is not identity. On the other hand, if what we normally speak of as ethical 'knowing' has a close similarity to knowledge that something is the case, this greatly strengthens the case for regarding it as legitimate to speak of ethical 'knowledge', and for regarding ethics as 'cognitive'.

In developing my argument, I shall assume (with one qualification, which I shall mention) the correctness of the careful and well-argued analysis of knowledge that something is the case which Ayer provided in *The Problem of Knowledge*. He there asserts that 'the necessary and sufficient conditions for knowing that something is the case are first that what one be said to know be true, secondly that one be sure of it, and thirdly that one have the right to be sure'.[1] He says of the right to be sure, 'This right may be earned in various ways.'[2]

Let us see whether conditions which are like Ayer's three conditions for knowledge that something is the case govern what we speak of as ethical 'knowledge'. We may use the four examples given at the beginning of the chapter. They are various enough so that if conditions like Ayer's three conditions govern what we would normally speak of as ethical 'knowledge' in these four cases, this would indicate that conditions like Ayer's three conditions pretty generally govern what we speak of as ethical 'knowledge'.

Something very much like Ayer's first condition appears to be a requirement for ethical 'knowledge' in all four cases. We speak of 'knowledge' only if we accept the correctness of what is said to be known. No one who believes that theft is in general right is going to credit Jones with knowledge that theft is in general wrong. No one who believes that it is right to imprison debtors is going to credit Smith with knowledge that he ought not to imprison Brown. No one who thinks that White is wrong about Green is going to

---

[1] *The Problem of Knowledge* (Harmondsworth: Penguin Books, 1956), p. 35.
[2] *loc. cit.*

say that White knows that Green is not really a bad person. And no one who considers a contemplative life to be worthless is going to credit Black with knowledge that it is highly desirable. In each case, to speak of knowledge implies that the ethical claim in question is correct.

Something like Ayer's second condition also appears to be a requirement for what we normally speak of as 'knowledge' in all four cases. We speak of 'knowledge' only if a man believes confidently what he is said to know. We normally would say unhesitatingly that Jones knows that theft is in general wrong. But we would not say this (in what has been distinguished as an ethical sense) if Jones does not believe confidently that theft is in general wrong. Let us suppose that Jones, after he refuses to steal the art object, says he acted mainly on impulse, and says furthermore that he has half a mind to believe that he acted foolishly—the art object will do as much good in his possession as in anyone else's. It now seems conceivable to him, he says, that theft is often not really wrong. We would then hesitate to say that Jones believed confidently that theft is in general wrong, and would be correspondingly hesitant to say (in an ethical sense) that he knew that theft is in general wrong. The degree of our hesitancy of course would depend in large part on how seriously we took Jones' remarks. Normally we assume that the belief that theft is in general wrong is deeply enough ingrained that any sane, well-bred adult, in a sober moment, would say 'Of course theft is in general wrong'. But if Jones really is not sure any more, then we would not say that (in an ethical sense) he knows that theft is in general wrong.

Similarly, if Smith is very much in doubt about the rightness of imprisoning debtors, and merely is inclined slightly to believe that he ought not to imprison Brown, we would normally not say that he knows that he ought not to imprison Brown. (He himself of course would probably deny that he 'knows' that he ought not to imprison Brown: 'I am not sure', he might say.) If White hesitantly judges that Green is not really a bad person, but is not really sure, we would not say that White knows that Green is not really a bad person. If Black is only slightly inclined to say that the contemplative life is highly desirable, and still feels grave doubts, we would not say that Black knows that the contemplative life is highly desirable.

There is one qualification on all of this. There is a sense of 'know' in which we often say of a person that he knows something even when he is uncertain. This is when we feel that in a calm moment he should be able to recognize, on the basis of what he already believes or has been informed of, the obvious truth (or correctness) of whatever it is. In a sense like this we say 'Deep down he knows . . .'. In this sense we might say to Jones, even if Jones is genuinely uncertain about the wrongness of stealing the art object, 'Look, you know that it would be wrong to steal that'; we might say to a third person 'Of course he knows that it would be wrong; it is just that he is confused.' In this sense also, we might say, if we felt that Smith ought readily (on the basis of beliefs he already held, information he already had, etc.) in a calm moment to recognize the wrongness of imprisoning debtors, 'He *knows* that he ought not to imprison Brown', even if he were about to have Brown imprisoned.

It is worth pointing out (my one qualification on Ayer's account) that there is a parallel sense of 'know' with regard to non-ethical knowledge. If someone who has lived in Massachusetts for many years says that Springfield is the capital of Massachusetts, we might say 'You know it is Boston.' Someone hesitating over a calculation might be told 'You know that nine times six is fifty-four.' An economist who is hesitating in predicting the effects of a financial policy might be told by a colleague 'You know that Gresham's Law applies in this situation.'

In the sense of 'know' which Ayer analyses, of course, the economist does not know that Gresham's Law applies if he has not figured it out, and a man does not know that Boston is the capital of Massachusetts if he has forgotten it. But in a parallel sense to Ayer's, if Smith decides that it would be right to imprison Brown then he does not know that he ought not to imprison Brown.

Something very much like Ayer's third condition appears to be a requirement for what we normally speak of as 'knowledge' (in an ethical sense) in all four cases. We speak of 'knowledge' only if we grant the right to be confident. This right, like Ayer's 'right to be sure', may be variously earned.

I pointed out in Chapter VI that there are many cases in which we consider that experience confers the right to be confident of an ethical judgment. Examples 3 and 4 are such cases. White has a right to be confident of his judgment which an inexperienced, untrained person who independently (without having noticed anything about Green which he could cite as relevant to his judgment) made the same judgment would not have. We would not speak of such a person as 'knowing' that Green was not really a bad person, even if we acknowledged that his judgment was correct. Similarly, someone who made the same judgment as Black, and who could appeal neither to experience, reasons, or good authority, would scarcely be said to 'know' that the contemplative life is highly desirable, even by someone who agreed with his judgment.

As I have pointed out, authority sometimes may substitute for experience. If White really is thoroughly reliable, we may know on the authority of White that Green is not really a bad person. On the other hand, if Black has no unusual claim to respect, it would be quite odd to speak of knowing the desirability of the contemplative life on the authority of Black. Whether Black's claim is correct is a difficult enough matter so that we would hope to have more of a basis for confidence. Suppose however that Y says 'I know that the contemplative life is highly desirable'; we ask 'How do you know?'; and Y replies 'Aristotle says so, and I find his account of the advantages of the contemplative life to be quite convincing.' Here many of us, who feel strongly convinced that the contemplative life is highly desirable, and that Aristotle gives a good account of it, might well say 'Y knows that the contemplative life is highly desirable.'

Authority, as I have pointed out, gives Jones a right to be confident that theft is in general wrong, a right shared by all members of society. Reasoning gives Smith a right to be confident of his judgment. We would normally, given the conditions of the example, speak of him as 'knowing' that he ought not to have Brown imprisoned; but if the case were different, in that he could give no reasoning on which his judgment were based and also could not cite relevant experiences of the effects of imprisoning debtors or appeal to adequate authority, we would not speak of him as 'knowing' that he ought not to imprison Brown.

It is true, on the other hand, that if we agree that Jones, Smith, White and Black have made correct judgments, confidently believe what they say, and have (on some basis or other) a right to be confident, we will normally speak of them as 'knowing' (in what I have distinguished as an ethical sense) that which they claim. Thus there appears to be a fairly close parallel between necessary and sufficient conditions governing our ordinary use of 'know' in an ethical sense, and the necessary and sufficient conditions which Ayer states for knowledge that something is the case. Three conditions similar to Ayer's are sufficient in ethical cases. These conditions also are necessary, with one qualification: I have pointed out a sense in which we sometimes speak of someone as having ethical 'knowledge' even when he is not sure of a judgment. However I have pointed out that there is a parallel to this qualification in relation to knowledge that something is the case.

This suggests a close family resemblance between our ordinary ethical use of 'know' and our ordinary use of 'know' in relation to what is the case. It is worth stressing again that this close resemblance is not identity, nor is it complete. I have suggested that in most normal contexts 'true' is less at home in relation to ethical claims than in relation to claims that something is the case. Clearly also some of the conditions under which someone will have the right to be confident of an ethical claim will differ markedly from conditions which govern one's right to be sure of a claim that something is the case. Furthermore, as my discussion of ethical hypocrisy had suggested, what is involved in believing an ethical claim confidently is not entirely comparable to what is involved in feeling sure of a claim that something is the case.

Nevertheless it is striking how similar a formula to Ayer's can be fitted to our ordinary ethical use of 'know'. We can see from this that it is no accident that we do normally use 'know' in an ethical sense. 'Knowledge' cannot be defined: the use of this term, like the use of other general terms, is a matter of family resemblances. And the conditions which surround some ethical judgments have a strong family resemblance to the conditions under which we say that someone who judges that something is the case knows that it is the case. This suggests indeed that, even if for some reason we all stopped using 'know' in an ethical sense, it would be logical to begin again.

The point may be put this way. It makes sense to speak of ethical knowledge, not only because in fact we do, but also because some ethical judgments fulfil conditions which are closely similar to the conditions which other kinds of judgments have to fulfil in order for us to speak of the person who makes them as having knowledge. It is not only on the surface that ordinary language indicates the existence of ethical knowledge.

III

Thus far I have shown that both the surface and the deeper levels of ordinary language allow us to speak of ethical knowledge. There is nothing in what we have uncovered which suggests that ordinary language is confused in this. There is a great deal to suggest that 'non-cognitivist' ethical philosophies would have to influence ordinary language very deeply and thoroughly in order to make it seem quite odd to use 'know' in an ethical sense. Indeed, even if 'non-cognitivist' philosophers were to work such deep changes in our ordinary language patterns, one could introduce adequately the concept of ethical knowledge simply by stipulating that 'know' (in an ethical sense) means what it did in the mid-twentieth century. One could continue to speak of ethical knowledge in much the way in which one can still speak Latin.

There remain ethical and philosophical objections against speaking of ethical knowledge. Both demand close attention; but a philosopher who is unaided by sympathetic teams of psychologists and sociologists is probably in less of a position to deal with the former than with the latter. I shall say what I can with regard to the ethical objections, and then move on to the philosophical objections.

The ethical objections mentioned at the end of Chapter III and in Chapter V can be derived from Olafson and from the remarks of anthropologists such as Ruth Benedict and Melville Hershkovits. Olafson suggests that if we adopt a meta-ethics like Stevenson's we will conceive of our moral judgment as 'no longer a kind of witnessing or reporting', but rather as 'a kind of doing'.[1] This Olafson appears to regard as a good thing. Mrs Benedict, Hershkovits, and the dwindling band of cultural relativists among anthropologists, clearly feel that to adopt a relativistic way of speaking would help to emancipate us from 'ethnocentrism', and might well make us more tolerant.

In Chapter V, I argued at length that one need not be a relativist to be tolerant; indeed there is no great difficulty in believing that there is ethical knowledge, and still being tolerant. Furthermore, I argued that relativism does encourage people to be tolerant to a fault. Perhaps more important than either of these points, however, is that there is no solid evidence which gives any strong indication that espousing a relativistic philosophy leads to practical advantages. Thus, all things considered, it is hard to see why we should abandon our ordinary patterns of language in favour of a relativistic way of talking.

[1] 'Meta-Ethics and the Moral Life', *Philosophical Review*, Vol. LXV (1956), p. 174.

Olafson's points are far more ingenious and subtle than those of the cultural relativists, but some similar objections can be raised. Someone who adopted my view of the relation between ethical knowledge and conduct could very well think of his ethical judgments as 'a kind of doing' as well as 'a kind of witnessing'. This perhaps is not quite what Olafson would hope for; but it can be argued that it combines the best of both worlds: incorporating from the old moral world the notion that ethical judgment involves responsibility to standards, or to whatever ought to affect our judgment, and incorporating from the world of Stevenson the idea that ethical judgment is not an entirely theoretic activity. Again, also, there is a lack of solid evidence as to what the effects of shifting to an emotivist meta-ethic would be.

The philosophical objections to speaking of ethical knowledge loom much larger than the ethical objections. We have discussed some of the philosophical objections, most notably in Chapter IV: we may now give them final consideration. If it turns out that neither the ethical nor the philosophical objections to speaking of ethical knowledge appear very strong, this, added to the fact that we do ordinarily speak of ethical knowledge, and that to speak of ethical knowledge fits the patterns of our ordinary use of 'know', shows that there is a very strong case for saying that there is ethical knowledge.

There are two especially pressing philosophical objections against saying that there is ethical knowledge. The first is that the only claims which may be 'cognitive' are those which have 'literal meaning', which in turn are those which are analytic or are subject to empirical verification. Irreducibly ethical claims ('actual' ethical claims, in Ayer's terminology) do not belong in either category, and hence are not 'cognitive'. The second (which lends some support to the first) is that disagreement about ethical claims is very prevalent, and there appears no sound method for finally settling such disagreement. If there is ethical knowledge, the objector may inquire, who is it who has it? Aristotle or Epicurus? Queen Victoria or the Marquis de Sade?

I have indicated in Chapter IV that the first objection, at least as it may be found in *Language Truth and Logic*, rests on important unargued assumptions. Why assume that the only genuine verification of non-analytic claims is 'empirical verification'? Why force all non-analytic claims to lie in a Procrustean bed designed for the sciences?

There is another flaw in Ayer's position, which the discussion in Chapters VI and VII allows us to see. *Language Truth and Logic*, like most presentations of extremist positions, draws a picture in black and white. One one side are analytic statements and those statements capable of empirical verification: thoroughly contrasted to these are all other kinds of claims, which lack 'literal meaning'.

We are now in a position to have a better view than this. Ethical claims may not be analytic or, very strictly speaking, capable of empirical verification; but they also are not thoroughly removed from logic or from empirical evidence. A broad picture of logic, and of the varieties of experience, allows us to see that the differences between ethics and what Ayer considers literally meaningful are a matter of shadings, not of sharp contrasts.

As I pointed out in Chapter VI, many ethical judgments are arrived at as a result of experience, and may even function as reports of that experience. It is perfectly in order to say that one has seen the emptiness of a certain mode of life, or has seen how wrong it is to steal the savings of a poor man. Empirical evidence also plainly is relevant to the question of whether poor people in Mississippi should be given more food ('What will happen if they are not given more food?' we will want to ask), and the question of whether Jones is really a good man.

In many cases, of course, ethical experience has a 'personal' quality, and is less liable to be shared (at least in our society) than most of the experiences relevant to the results of laboratory experiments. In many cases, also, there will not be very general agreement as to just how experience is to count in relation to an ethical judgment. If experience tells us that malnutrition will become widespread unless poor people in Mississippi are given more food, some people will count that more heavily than others will in support of deciding that one ought to give the food. For these reasons, it would be misleading to speak of ethical judgments as being able to be empirically verified. But the reader ought now to be in a position to see that it would be even more misleading to set up a simple contrast between ethical judgments and judgments which can be empirically verified. If the worst sort of metaphysical rhapsody is black, and empirically verifiable propositions are white, then a great many ethical claims are a very light gray. It is especially important to point this out in view of the fact that sometimes scientific hypotheses (in cases in which it is not entirely clear how much weight certain kinds of evidence will have in confirming or disconfirming the hypothesis) arguably also are a very light gray.

As very many writers, notably Hare, Toulmin and Baier, have pointed out, logical argument also may play an important role in ethics. This does not mean that ethical claims are logical claims: I have argued, indeed, that Baier makes ethical claims seem more like logical claims than they really are. But, on the other hand, ethical claims are not totally unlike logical claims; and logic plays as important and central a role in ethics as it does in the sciences. Ethical judgments, after all, may be 'sound', 'well-based' and 'reasoned'; ethical judgments, in point of fact, often are arrived at as a result of careful rational argument. In view of this, while it would be highly misleading to speak of ethical judgments as analytic (and none of the philosophers I have just mentioned does this), it also is misleading to set up an extreme contrast between ethical judgments and judgments which are analytic. The logic of ethical argument often is not traditional deductive logic, and logical arguments are not decisive in ethical matters in the straightforward way that they would be in a purely logical investigation. But, equally, many ethical judgments are quite different from unreasoned pronouncements which lack logical support.

The point that I have been getting at is this. In view of the roles of experience and reason in ethics, we may say that very many ethical claims have characteristics which are like the characteristics which *Language Truth and Logic* requires for literal meaning. We may go so far as to say that they are much more like Ayer's required characteristics than they are unlike them. Thus, even if we were to assume that Ayer was after all pointing in the right direction, we can see the possibility of 'liberalizing' his requirements. It is of course open to Ayer to draw his requirements for literal meaning very narrowly. But now at least we are in a position to see how narrow the formulation of *Language Truth and Logic* is. Considering the close relevance of empirical and logical factors to ethical claims, and considering also the patterns to be found in ordinary language, we ourselves may want to speak of ethical claims as 'literally meaningful', and to speak of ethics as 'cognitive'. Certainly there is no drastic opposition between ethical claims and those claims which Ayer calls literally meaningful which compels us to do otherwise.

The second philosophical objection is the one which I think would be most commonly raised today. In Chapter IV, I pointed out that its basis is a contingent fact: the fact there there is more ethical diversity than there is diversity concerning our judgments of what is immediately perceivable. One can imagine a society in which things are very different, in which people very generally 'see things the same way' in ethical matters, but constantly are involved in endless disputes about the presence of elephants and apparitions of the Virgin. Thus ethical diversity is simply a fact about our world, and not a necessary consequence of differences between ethical and scientific discourse. I pointed out also that the judgment that there is, say, no elephant in this room is no more capable of strict logical proof than is any ethical judgment.

Remembering these two points should have a therapeutic effect on any tendency to dismiss claims to ethical knowledge because of ethical diversity. There is one further point which ought to be made now. This is that, even within our increasingly fragmented society, it is possible to exaggerate the amount of ethical disagreement. There is great disagreement concerning the desirability of the contemplative life, and the wrongness of abortion; but on the whole there seems little disagreement concerning the desirability of having adequate food, or the wrongness of poisoning one's enemies. On these latter matters there probably is not a greater number of stubborn dissenters than remain with regard to Darwin's Theory of Evolution: indeed there may well be more dissent concerning evolution than concerning the wrongness of poisoning one's enemies.

Now there is a genuine relation between the amount of consensus which surrounds a view and one's right to claim knowledge that the view is correct. It is this: where intelligent men differ it is, or ought to be, harder to feel sure or confident of the correct answer. Because of this, less is required for one to have a right to be sure (or confident) of a matter about which everyone agrees than is required to have a right to be sure (or confident) of a matter about which there is great diversity of opinion. We have little hesitation about according the right to be confident that murder is wrong. But we might feel that the division of opinions concerning the wrongness of abortion indicates that there is a great deal of room for doubt, and accordingly (if we are impressed by this, and do not consider the correct answer obvious) we may hesitate to say that anyone knows either that abortion is always wrong or that abortion is sometimes justified. Cromwell's words to the Scotch Presbyterians, 'I beseech you, in the bowels of Christ, think it possible you may be mistaken', plainly have more weight addressed to someone who proclaims the wrongness of abortion than to someone who proclaims the wrongness of murder.

This does not mean that it is impossible to know, say, that abortion is not always wrong. Those of us who are firmly convinced, on the basis of considerations regarding the health of an expectant mother etc. that abortion sometimes is justified, would certainly say that someone who had carefully reasoned out the matter, and shared our conclusion, knows that in some cases abortion is justified. The point is simply that especially careful thought, and good grounds, are required for 'knowledge' in a case in which there are major differences of opinion. Also, of course, in such a case there will be a corresponding diversity of opinion concerning claims to knowledge. No one who believes that abortion is always wrong will ever speak of someone as 'knowing' that abortion is sometimes justified. But it is worth reminding ourselves that no one who rejects Darwin's theory will ever speak of someone as 'knowing' that man has evolved from lower animals.

I owe the example of Darwin's theory to Vincent Tomas, who argues that 'not all disagreements in belief occur between people who are tacitly agreed as to how the disagreement should be settled'.[1] The great controversy over Darwin's theory was kept alive, he says, by the fact that some people did not accept the criteria for a solution accepted by the other side. Some people, that is, did not consider the results of the scientific method to have as much weight as the testimony of the Bible.

Now a controversy of this sort can be spoken of as 'settled', even if a poll tomorrow were to disclose that fifty per cent of the population still believe that Darwin's theory is false. It is settled because there is a consensus among those people whom we regard as intelligent and competent in such matters. But why should we not, then, equally say that it is settled that it is wrong publicly to torture criminals, even if there are still some sadists who believe differently?

It is impossible to provide a deductive argument which amounts to strict proof that the results of the scientific method outweigh the testimony of the Bible. Thus it is impossible to provide strict proof that Darwin's theory is correct; for that matter, it is impossible to provide strict proof that it is wrong publicly to torture criminals. But surely anyone who rejects the arguments supporting Darwin's theory, or the arguments showing what a bad thing it is publicly to torture criminals, is simply unreasonable. After all, Darwin's theory rests on statements about fossil remains etc.; the view that it is wrong publicly to torture criminals rests on statements about the

[1] 'Ethical Disagreements', *Mind*, Vol. LX (1951), p. 210.

undesirability of pain and brutality etc.; and in both cases the supporting statements have, to use a phrase of Nelson Goodman's, high 'initial credibility'.[1]

Someone may ask 'If there is knowledge about man's origins, who has it, Darwin or a fundamentalist who accepts the literal truth of the *Genesis* account?' I think that almost all of us would answer 'Darwin', even if there is no strict logical proof of this, and even if many people turned out to take the side of the fundamentalist. Similarly, if someone asks 'If there is knowledge concerning the rightness or wrongness of public torture of criminals, who has it, Queen Victoria or the Marquis de Sade (assuming that the Marquis de Sade really did believe in public torture)?' the answer surely is 'Queen Victoria'. (We might say 'Queen Victoria was wrong about a lot of things, but she knew that public torture of criminals was wrong.') We cannot prove this; sadists may disagree; but why should such factors deter us from speaking of knowledge if they did not deter us in the case of Darwin?

There is an obvious reply: namely that Darwin's theory, while it is incapable of strict proof, is supported by considerable scientific evidence. But the claim that it is wrong publicly to torture criminals also is supported by considerable evidence. There is evidence concerning the effect of such spectacles on the state of mind and future behaviour of men who would be subjected to it, and on the attitude of the public towards violence and pain. A penologist might even call much of this evidence 'scientific'. It is hard to dismiss the support which this evidence gives to the claim that it is wrong publicly to torture criminals.

A reasonable conclusion is, then, that sometimes we can tell who has ethical knowledge. On the subject of torture, Queen Victoria had it rather than the Marquis de Sade. On the question of whether the avoidance of pain is in general a more important goal than that of exercising a variety of virtues, most of us would agree that Aristotle had knowledge. ('Aristotle knew', we might say, 'that the most desirable way of life involves the functioning of both moral and intellectual virtues.')

Of course ethical problems sometimes are more tangled and difficult than factual problems, and of course our temperament and social background very often has a much greater influence on our

---

[1] 'Sense and Certainty', *Philosophical Review*, Vol. LXI (1952), pp. 162–3. Cf. also Israel Scheffler, *Science and Subjectivity* (New York: Bobbs Merrill, 1967), Chapter V.

answers to ethical questions than on our answers to factual questions. Of course, also, attitudes and performances are intimately connected with ethical judgment, as I hope my discussion of hypocrisy showed.

A great deal of what philosophers like Stevenson said is true and important. Nevertheless we can quarrel with what they have made of it. It remains the case that we ordinarily speak often of ethical judgments as being right, wrong, correct and incorrect, in an unqualified sense which is irreducibly ethical. (Someone who approves of torture is wrong, even if this intimately involves the fact that he has the wrong attitude.) It remains the case that the existence of ethical knowledge is implicit in our ordinary ethical discourse, for reasons which go deep into the structure of our discourse. No philosophical objections to the claim that there is ethical knowledge have succeeded in pointing out a contrast between what is said to be ethical 'knowledge' and other forms of knowledge which is so thorough as to make it seem absurd to speak of ethical knowledge.

My arguments may not have convinced every reader; but even so, they will have had some success if they give the reader a clearer view of the problem of ethical knowledge. After all, it is desirable to have a clear view of such an important philosophical problem. The reader presumably knows this.

INDEX

GEORGE ALLEN & UNWIN LTD

Head office:
40 Museum Street, London, W.C.1
Telephone: 01–405 8577

Sales, Distribution and Accounts Departments
Park Lane, Hemel Hempstead, Herts.
Telephone: 0442 3244

Athens: 7 Stadiou Street, Athens 125
Auckland: P.O. Box 36013, Northcote, Auckland 9
Barbados: P.O. Box 222, Bridgetown
Beirut: Deeb Building, Jeanne d'Arc Street
Bombay: 103/5 Fort Street, Bombay 1
Calcutta: 285J Bepin Behari Ganguli Street, Calcutta 12
P.O. Box 2314 Joubert Park, Johannesburg, South Africa
Dacca: Alico Building, 18 Motijheel, Dacca 2
Delhi: B 1/18 Asaf Ali Road, New Delhi 1
Ibadan: P.O. Box 62
Karachi: Karachi Chambers, McLeod Road
Lahore: 22 Falettis' Hotel, Egerton Road
Madras: 2/18 Mount Road, Madras 2
Manila: P.O. Box 157, Quezon City, D-502
Mexico: Liberia Britanica, S.A. Separos Rendor 125, Mexico 4DF
Nairobi: P.O. Box 30583
Ontario: 2330 Midland Avenue, Agincourt
Rio de Janeiro: Caixa Postal 2537-Zc-00
Singapore: 248c-6 Orchard Road, Singapore 9
Sydney: N.S.W.: Bradbury House, 55 York Street
Tokyo: C.P.O. Box 1728, Tokyo 100-91

ETHICS AND CHRISTIANITY

KEITH WARD

The book explores the logic of the Christian ethic in the light of contemporary moral philosophy. It provides a philosophical foundation for discussion between philosophers and theologians.

Part One explains the objective and attitudinal nature of Christian ethics—its claim that morality is based on the will of God, which demands the realization of specific human attitudes. Part Two elaborates on the claim that Christian morality is authoritative, that Christ is a unique moral authority. The notions of moral knowledge, vocation and agape are examined, and ways of assessing specific Christian claims are suggested. Part Three deals with the teleological and charismatic elements of Christian morality, its hope for a future consummation and its offer of forgiveness and grace. The notions of sin, grace, Heaven and Hell are discussed, and the doctrine of desert is rejected as incompatible with Christian teaching.

Keith Ward who is Lecturer in Moral Philosophy at the University of St. Andrew's was author of *Fifty Key Words in Philosophy*.

Demy 8vo 288 pages

OUR KNOWLEDGE OF RIGHT AND WRONG

JONATHAN HARRISON

This is a sustained critical examination of recent ethical philosophy. It is the longest and most comprehensive consideration of the subject of right and wrong in the English language.

The first part of the book considers various traditional attempts to solve this problem: for example, objectivism, subjectivism, intuitionism, naturalism, evolutionary theories, and non-cognitivism. In the second part the author makes his own attempt at an informal solution, writing with a distinctive and positive approach.

Demy 8vo 424 pages

ASCENT TO THE ABSOLUTE
METAPHYSICAL PAPERS AND LECTURES
J. N. FINDLAY

These lectures and papers are all concerned, directly or indirectly, with an 'Absolute Theory', the theory of an unique, necessary Existent, in some manner differentiated in empirical contents and explanatory of contigent matters of fact, yet itself basically characterized by non-empirical properties, all necessary but not trivially so.

Once the notion of an Absolute is tentatively entertained, it opens up a fascinating line of conceptual research in which new notions and principles will constantly come to light. This line of research will not necessarily lead to one or other of a theistic or pantheistic or metaphysical Absolutes of the past.

Professor Findlay is Clark Professor of Moral Philosophy and Metaphysics at Yale University. His other writings in the *Muirhead Library of Philosophy Series* are *Hegel: A Re-Examination*, *Values and Intentions*, *The Discipline of the Cave* and *The Transcendence of the Cave*.

Demy 8vo   272 pages

CONTEMPORARY AMERICAN PHILOSOPHY
EDITED BY J. E. SMITH

This is a collection of fourteen essays by American philosophers on topics at present being discussed in America.

Naturalism and Idealism, personalism and pragmatism, analysis and speculative philosophy are all represented, and the ideas of junior as well as senior philosophers are included.

These essays not only show the pluralism of American thought, but also reveal the capacity of American thinkers to learn from other philosophical traditions.

Demy 8vo   400 pages

REASON AND SCEPTICISM

MICHAEL A. SLOTE

This work rebuts Wittgensteinian and Phenomenalist attempts to overcome epistemological scepticism and provides powerful new arguments for the scientific reasonableness of belief in an external world.

Professor Slote argues that it is reasonable to accept the 'hypothesis' of an external world that is and has been as it seems to be. A new form of the 'argument of analogy' is employed to establish the existence of other minds and unobserved objects, and is defended from various objections. And sceptical challenges to scientific methodology—among them Goodman's *New Riddle of Introduction*, are examined and answered.

The professor discusses scepticism about the existence of God and illuminates certain previously ignored *rational* but *non-scientific* grounds for belief in a deity.

Demy 8vo   240 pages

HYPOTHESIS AND PERCEPTION

ERROL HARRIS

The author in this sequel to *The Foundations of Metaphysics in Science* develop a new theory of scientific method, quite opposed to that of Carnap, Reichenbach, Hempel and Nagel. The empiricist theory is shown to be internally incoherent. It also proves to be unsupported by comparison with actual scientific practice.

Demy 8vo   416 pages

THE PERSON GOD IS

PETER A. BERTOCCI

The contention of this book is that it is only a radical experientialism which can inform reasonable hypotheses about God. God as a person must not be made to fit into prior physiological, psychological, sociological, and theological conceptions, nor circumscribed by any methodology that neglects any dimension of human experience.

Demy 8vo   352 pages.

LONDON · GEORGE ALLEN & UNWIN LTD